BARRON'S BOOK NOTES

RICHARD WRIGHT'S

Native Son &
Black Boy

BARRON'S BOOK NOTES

RICHARD WRIGHT'S

Native Son & Black Boy

BY

Michael Gallantz
Communications Program
School of Business Administration
University of California at Berkeley

SERIES COORDINATOR
Murray Bromberg
Principal, Wang High School of Queens
Holliswood, New York
Past President
High School Principals Association of New York City

BARRON'S EDUCATIONAL SERIES, INC.
Woodbury, New York • London • Toronto • Sydney

All inquiries should be addressed to:
Barron's Educational Series, Inc.
113 Crossways Park Drive
Woodbury, New York 11797

Library of Congress Catalog Card No. 85-26882

International Standard Book No. 0-8120-3529-1

Library of Congress Cataloging-in-Publication Data
Gallantz, Michael.
  Richard Wright's Native son & Black boy.

  (Barron's book notes)
  Bibliography: p. 129
  1. Wright, Richard, 1908–1960—Criticism and inter-
pretation.   2. Afro-Americans in literature.   I. Title.
II. Title: Richard Wright's Native son and Black boy.
III. Series.
PS3545.R815Z663   1986   813'.52   85-26882
ISBN 0-8120-3529-1

CONTENTS

ADVISORY BOARD

We wish to thank the following educators who helped us focus our *Book Notes* series to meet student needs and critiqued our manuscripts to provide quality materials.

Sandra Dunn, English Teacher
Hempstead High School, Hempstead, New York

Lawrence J. Epstein, Associate Professor of English
Suffolk County Community College, Selden, New York

Leonard Gardner, Lecturer, English Department
State University of New York at Stony Brook

Beverly A. Haley, Member, Advisory Committee
National Council of Teachers of English Student
Guide Series, Fort Morgan, Colorado

Elaine C. Johnson, English Teacher
Tamalpais Union High School District
Mill Valley, California

Marvin J. LaHood, Professor of English
State University of New York College at Buffalo

Robert Lecker, Associate Professor of English
McGill University, Montréal, Québec, Canada

David E. Manly, Professor of Educational Studies
State University of New York College at Geneseo

Bruce Miller, Associate Professor of Education
State University of New York at Buffalo

Frank O'Hare, Professor of English and
Director of Writing
Ohio State University, Columbus, Ohio

Faith Z. Schullstrom, Member, Executive Committee
National Council of Teachers of English
Director of Curriculum and Instruction
Guilderland Central School District, New York

Mattie C. Williams, Director, Bureau of Language Arts
Chicago Public Schools, Chicago, Illinois

HOW TO USE THIS BOOK

You have to know how to approach literature in order to get the most out of it. This *Barron's Book Notes* volume follows a plan based on methods used by some of the best students to read a work of literature.

Begin with the guide's section on the author's life and times. As you read, try to form a clear picture of the author's personality, circumstances, and motives for writing the work. This background usually will make it easier for you to hear the author's tone of voice, and follow where the author is heading.

Then go over the rest of the introductory material—such sections as those on the plot, characters, setting, themes, and style of the work. Underline, or write down in your notebook, particular things to watch for, such as contrasts between characters and repeated literary devices. At this point, you may want to develop a system of symbols to use in marking your text as you read. (Of course, you should only mark up a book you own, not one that belongs to another person or a school.) Perhaps you will want to use a different letter for each character's name, a different number for each major theme of the book, a different color for each important symbol or literary device. Be prepared to mark up the pages of your book as you read. Put your marks in the margins so you can find them again easily.

Now comes the moment you've been waiting for—the time to start reading the work of literature. You may want to put aside your *Barron's Book Notes* volume until you've read the work all the way through. Or you may want to alternate, reading the *Book Notes* analysis of each section as soon as you have finished reading the corresponding part of the original. Before you move on, reread crucial passages you don't fully understand. (Don't take this guide's analysis for granted—make up your own mind as to what the work means.)

Once you've finished the whole work of literature, you may want to review it right away, so you can firm up your ideas about what it means. You may want to leaf through the book concentrating on passages you marked in reference to one character or one theme. This is also a good time to reread the *Book Notes* introductory material, which pulls together insights on specific topics.

When it comes time to prepare for a test or to write a paper, you'll already have formed ideas about the work. You'll be able to go back through it, refreshing your memory as to the author's exact words and perspective, so that you can support your opinions with evidence drawn straight from the work. Patterns will emerge, and ideas will fall into place; your essay question or term paper will almost write itself. Give yourself a dry run with one of the sample tests in the guide. These tests present both multiple-choice and essay questions. An accompanying section gives answers to the multiple-choice questions as well as suggestions for writing the essays. If you have to select a term paper topic, you may choose one from the list of suggestions in this book. This guide also provides you with a reading list, to help you when you start research for a term paper, and a selection of provocative comments by critics, to spark your thinking before you write.

THE AUTHOR AND HIS TIMES

After Bigger Thomas, the central character of the novel *Native Son*, has "murdered a white girl and cut her head off and burnt her body," he thinks that he has "created a new life for himself. It was something that was all his own, and it was the first time in his life he had had anything that others could not take from him." Richard Wright could well have felt the same way about the quiet, creative act of writing *Native Son* as that novel's protagonist felt about his bloody act of violence. Wright had grown up poor and lonely, without a stable family life, a regular education, or a solid community of friends. Until he was in his late twenties, no one took his ambitions seriously. But *Native Son* gave Wright "new life" as a financially secure and internationally famous author. And, unlike the brief sense of power that came from Bigger's physical expression of anger, the changes resulting from Wright's literary expression of the same emotion were permanent.

Some of Wright's early background resembles Bigger's. Like Bigger, he was brought up without a father; like Bigger's family, Wright's also left the South for the urban ghetto of Chicago; like Bigger, whose schooling only went as far as the eighth grade, Wright's finished with the ninth, and like his fictional creation, the author of *Native Son* grew up a loner and a rebel, whose devoutly religious family thought him a candidate for a life of crime.

And Richard Wright's life affected his writing in two more fundamental ways as well. He was often a victim of the white world's hostility to blacks; as a result many of his books, including *Native Son*, portray both racial discrimination and the black response to that injustice. Similarly, even as an adult, Wright frequently felt isolated, from blacks as well as from whites, and several of his major characters share this sense of being separate and alone.

Wright was born on September 4, 1908, in a tenant farmer's cabin in the hamlet of Roxie, Mississippi. His father, Nathaniel, was a son of one of the few local freedmen to have retained the small farm he had acquired after the Civil War. But because Nathaniel deserted the family when Richard was five, his mother, Ella Wilson Wright, was by far the more important parent to him. Unlike Nathaniel, Ella was from the middle class and had acquired an education. She had been a schoolteacher, but she gave up that profession to help Nathaniel with his farming. After Nathaniel left her, she worked as a maid until a paralytic stroke made her and her children dependent on the support of Ella's own parents and siblings.

In *Black Boy*, an account of his childhood and youth, Wright says his mother's suffering was one of the major influences on his developing personality. But he experienced much pain of his own too. His family was so poor that Wright was often acutely hungry, and the Wrights moved so frequently that he never put down sustained roots in one community. He also felt oppressed by his maternal grandmother's stern religion, which led her to ban fiction from the household because she regarded it as the work of the devil. With his mother severely ill, Wright found little sympathy or understanding at home and was usually quite lonely.

Wright also chafed under the racial hostility that he experienced. After the Civil War, the South had found ways of preventing the freed slaves from attaining equality. At the time Wright was growing up, Southern whites prevented blacks from voting, maintained separate and inferior educational institutions for them, tried to keep them from holding all but the most menial jobs, and insisted on their behaving deferentially in the presence of whites.

Such discriminatory practices directed against people of a particular color, ethnic background, or race are called "racist," as are the attitudes, ideas, and prejudices used to justify such unequal treatment. As Wright was to learn later, racism existed in the North as well as in the South. But in the South it was sanctioned by law, and it was more universally accepted and more severely applied. Blacks who violated the South's racial codes often faced violence, as did Wright's uncle, Silas "Buster" Hoskins, who was killed by whites who wanted to take over his business and property. Wright describes this incident and many of his later encounters with racism in Black Boy.

In 1925, after completing the ninth and final grade of the black public school in Jackson, Mississippi, Wright saved some money and left for Memphis, Tennessee, where he worked for an optical company. In Memphis, Wright discovered the angry journalism of H.L. Mencken, as well as the realistic novels of writers like Sinclair Lewis, Sherwood Anderson, and Theodore Dreiser. Wright had already learned to love fiction and had even written a story published in his local newspaper. But his interest had been adventure and escape stories. Mencken's bitter attacks on American institutions made Wright aware that words could be weapons, while Lewis's and Dreiser's realistic portraits of middle and working class life taught him that literature could help to understand the world, not just to escape from it.

The racism of Memphis was almost as oppressive to Wright as that of Mississippi. In a pattern continuing into his adulthood, he fled to hopefully freer territory, the Northern city of Chicago. Arriving in late 1927, Wright worked as a porter, dishwasher, substitute post office clerk, hospital orderly, and insurance salesman. This last job introduced him to many poor black households and gave him background information for *Native Son*. And, for a while, the Wrights, like Bigger's family, all shared one room.

As the Great Depression that began in 1929 threw Wright and millions of others out of work, radical political movements gained many new adherents. In 1933, Wright joined the John Reed Club, an organization of writers and artists who were members of or sympathizers with the Communist Party. One of the Chicago club's most active participants, Jan Wittenber, is thought to have become a model for *Native Son*'s Jan Erlone. The club strongly supported Wright's literary efforts, and he agreed with the Communists' call for unity among poor and working people of all races. *Left Front*, the Chicago club's magazine, published Wright's poetry, and only two months after joining, he was elected executive secretary. Shortly thereafter, Wright joined the Communist Party. He was soon writing poems and essays for national radical publications, such as *Anvil*, *New Masses*, *International Literature*, and *Partisan Review*. In 1935 the U.S. government set up a Federal Writers' Project to help unemployed writers, and the Illinois branch of the Project hired Wright and assigned him to the Federal Negro Theater. His literary skills were improving, and he began writing fiction, including some short stories about racial oppression and a humorous novel about Chicago blacks. Titled *Lawd Today*, the novel was not published until 1963, three years after his death.

In May 1937, Wright left Chicago for the nation's literary and publishing capital, New York City, where he became Harlem editor of the Communist Party's newspaper, the *Daily Worker*. Meanwhile, he was beginning to achieve broader renown. A novella he had submitted to a literary contest won first prize, and that story plus three earlier ones were published as *Uncle Tom's Children* (1938). Though it was well received and is still highly regarded by many critics, Wright thought the book was too sentimental. He wrote later that he decided to write something "so hard and deep" that readers "would have to face it without the consolation of tears."

That second book was *Native Son* (1940). An immediate best seller, it was also the major achievement of his career. Though Wright had expected *Native Son* to be controversial, the response of the white press was immediate, almost unanimous, and wildly enthusiastic. Perhaps the continuing economic crisis and the great popularity of John Steinbeck's social protest novels had created a more positive cultural climate than Wright had realized. Such influential newspapers and magazines as *The*

New York Times, the *New York Herald-Tribune*, *The New Yorker*, the *Saturday Review of Literature*, *The Nation*, the *New Republic*, *Newsweek*, and *Time* praised Wright's social analysis and his literary skill. Critics compared him to the famous American novelist Theodore Dreiser, to Steinbeck, and even to the great nineteenth-century novelists Charles Dickens and Fyodor Dostoevsky. The response from the black press was also favorable, though tempered with some criticism for his having chosen such a violent protagonist. And the reading public was as excited as the critics. *Native Son* sold some 200,000 copies in less than three weeks, a record for its publisher. Wright received a huge number of letters, the great majority of them praising the novel. Moreover, the South acclaimed the novel as highly as did the North. The city of Memphis, Tennessee, declared Wright its "adopted son," and after New York and Chicago, sales were best in Atlanta, Georgia, and Dallas and Houston, Texas. Almost overnight, Richard Wright had become one of the most famous writers in the United States.

A stage adaptation of *Native Son* played on Broadway in 1941, received enthusiastic reviews, and then toured several states; Wright had collaborated on the script. That same year Wright wrote the text for a photographic folk history of American blacks, *Twelve Million Black Voices*. In it Wright used the socialist ideas he had learned from his membership in the Communist Party and expressed them in emotional and poetic prose. He then wrote "The Man Who Lived Underground," a fable about a black man who hides in a sewer system. Foreshadowing some of his later work, it deemphasizes race and explores philosophical issues of freedom and social responsibility. Despite his fame, Wright was unable to get it published until 1944 and then only in part.

At odds with the Communist Party since 1942, Wright announced his final break with that organization in a 1944 *Atlantic Monthly* article, "I Tried to Be a Communist," later reprinted in *The God That Failed*, a collection of essays by ex-Communist writers. Though Wright's involvement in the Communist Party influenced the ideas that the characters Jan and Max present in *Native Son*, many readers have also found that novel to contain evidence of Wright's independence from the Communists. Indeed, the Party's reaction to the novel was mixed. When Wright joined the Communist Party, the Communists emphasized the struggle against racism. But especially after America's entry into World War II, they tended to deemphasize racial issues for fear that the fight for racial equality might undermine the unity needed for the war effort. This change in Party policy was one reason for Wright's disenchantment. But he also felt that the Party's insistence on participation in political organizing took time and energy away from writing and that the Party did not sufficiently respect its members' needs to develop as individuals.

Originally, "I Tried to Be a Communist" was to be the concluding section of Wright's autobiography. But *Black Boy* was published in 1945 without this account of his Chicago experiences. *Black Boy* became another best seller. Though its calmer prose and factual subject matter make it quite different from *Native Son*, the two are still regarded as Wright's most important works.

In 1946, Wright went to Paris and became friends

with some of France's leading intellectuals, especially the philosopher Jean-Paul Sartre and his followers. Because Wright felt that in France he could live free of the racial discrimination that still plagued him in the United States, in 1947 he settled in Paris permanently. Shortly thereafter, he began working on a movie version of *Native Son*. Wright wrote the screenplay and starred in the film, but in the United States censors insisted on cutting the picture severely, and it received poor reviews when it opened in 1951.

After this experience, Wright returned to composing novels. Sartre's philosophical emphasis on isolation and on individual freedom, appealed to him, and Sartre's ideas are thought to have influenced his next novel, *The Outsider* (1953). A philosophical tale plotted like a detective story, *The Outsider* rejects all forms of social pressure in favor of an extreme individualism. After *The Outsider*, Wright used a white hero to explore themes of guilt and violence in *Savage Holiday* (1954).

Wright was also becoming increasingly interested in the colonial world and in Africa especially. He spent the summer of 1953 in the British dependency known as the Gold Coast (now Ghana), and his experience in Africa formed the basis of several nonfiction attacks on colonialism, including *Black Power* (1954).

In the last years of his life, Wright returned to fiction. The subject matter of *The Long Dream* (1958), meant to be the first book of a trilogy, recalls *Black Boy*. It's a fictional account of a child growing up in Mississippi. The next year Wright fell ill with amoebic dysentery and never completely recovered. Nonetheless, he continued to write and lecture, and his health seemed to be improving until on November 28, 1960, he died of a sudden heart attack at the age of fifty-two.

Wright remains one of the most important Afro-American writers. Even black authors like James Baldwin and Ralph Ellison, who have found fault with him, nonetheless acknowledge Wright's deep influence on their careers. He helped them personally when they were beginning to write, and his success made theirs easier.

Wright's reputation in the United States declined after the 1940s, but it began to rise again during the political activism of the 1960s. Black political leaders like Malcolm X and Stokely Carmichael praised Wright, and Eldridge Cleaver, one of the major black writers to emerge from that period, said, "Of all American novelists of any hue, Richard Wright reigns supreme." Both Malcolm X's *Autobiography* and Cleaver's *Soul on Ice* pattern themselves after *Black Boy*'s autobiographical journey toward a clearer understanding of the world, and Ellison's *Invisible Man* shows *Black Boy*'s influence too. Meanwhile, Wright has affected works as diverse as French playwright Jean Genet's *The Blacks* and Truman Capote's murder story *In Cold Blood*. And many readers of all colors and political views still find *Native Son* and *Black Boy* compelling indictments of racism and penetrating character studies of individuals in revolt.

Native Son

THE NOVEL

The Plot

It's a typical morning in the one-room apartment where Bigger Thomas lives with his mother, younger brother, and sister in the central black section of Chicago. A foot-long rat has been terrifying the family, and Bigger traps and kills it. When he's done, his mother reminds him that he has a job interview that evening. She begs him to take the job. If he doesn't, the family will be dropped from public assistance.

Bigger goes to the pool hall to hang around with his buddies, Gus, Jack, and G.H. He suggests that the four rob Blum's Delicatessen. Though they have already committed several other petty robberies, Bigger's friends are afraid to steal from a white man. Bigger is scared too, but he won't admit it. So he backs out by picking a fight with Gus. Bigger decides never to return to the gang. He is looking forward to his new job.

Bigger's new employers, the Daltons, are a rich white family. Both their luxurious house and the Daltons themselves make Bigger feel fearful and extremely self-conscious. But he is hired as a chauffeur, and his first assignment is to take the Daltons' daughter Mary to her university class.

To Bigger's surprise, however, Mary does not want to go to the university. She asks him to drive her to meet her boyfriend and requests that he not tell anyone about this visit. Bigger is shocked to find out that Mary's boyfriend, Jan, is a Communist and that Mary is a Communist sympathizer. He has heard that Communists are crazy and violent. Both Jan and Mary insist that Bigger eat with them at a restaurant in his own neighborhood. Unaccustomed to such friendliness from whites, Bigger thinks they are ridiculing him. He feels ashamed and angry.

On the way home all three drink heavily. Jan gets out to catch a streetcar. When Bigger and Mary arrive at the Daltons', Mary is so drunk that Bigger has to carry her to her bedroom. Then Mary's blind mother comes in to check on her, and Bigger fears being discovered there. He holds a pillow over Mary's head to prevent her from making a sound. When Mrs. Dalton leaves, Bigger discovers he has killed Mary.

Fighting panic, he remembers that Mary was planning to leave for Detroit in the morning and hopes that the family will merely assume that she left early. He decides to burn her body in the furnace downstairs and has to cut her head off to make her fit.

The next morning Bigger starts to feel excited about the killing. Though it was accidental, he sees it as a defiance of the white people who have made him so miserable. Then he thinks of sending the Daltons a ransom note. Perhaps he can collect some money by making them think that Mary has been kidnapped. He tries to talk his girlfriend, Bessie, into helping, but she is afraid.

The Daltons are worried about Mary. Bigger has cleverly directed the investigators' suspicions to Jan and continues to do so by signing his ransom note "Red." The story is front-page news, and reporters crowd into the Dalton house.

No one thinks that a young, uneducated black man like Bigger would have had the intelligence or audacity to carry out such a plan. But the situation changes dramatically when one of the reporters discovers Mary's bones among the furnace ashes.

Now Bigger must flee. Because he fears that Bessie will betray him, he crushes her skull with a brick and leaves her to die in an abandoned building. Then, penniless, tired, hungry, and cold, Bigger flees from one empty building to another, while the Chicago police, searching door to door, close in on him. Finally, they capture Bigger on a rooftop.

The newspapers portray Bigger as a sex criminal, a primitive black man who raped and murdered a white woman. Bigger's mother's preacher advises him to pray to God and to turn to religion, a course Bigger rejects. Jan visits Bigger and urges him to defend himself with the aid of a Communist lawyer, Boris Max.

Bigger signs a confession, but Max, who has Bigger plead guilty, argues that the circumstances of Bigger's oppressed life justify a sentence of life imprisonment instead of death. As a mob outside demands Bigger's execution, the judge sentences him to the electric chair.

Knowing that he will die, Bigger's last desperate wish is to communicate his feelings to Max. He tells a shocked Max that his murders were meaningful acts that came from deep within. The two men say good-bye, and Bigger is left to face death alone.

The Characters

MAJOR CHARACTERS

Bigger Thomas

Bigger is a young black man who wants to be able to do all the things white people do but who knows he has no such chance. He is usually afraid, especially of humiliation. His ignorance and poverty make him ashamed, but he doesn't want to reveal either his shame or his fear because such a disclosure would be humiliating too. So Bigger keeps his feelings raging inside him, and he is furious at those who provoke these overwhelming emotions. He is especially furious at whites, not only because they are responsible for the oppressive conditions of his life but also because they scare and embarrass him. But he is also often angry at his fellow blacks, sometimes for their passivity and sometimes for their ability to see through his poses.

Bigger changes during the novel. After killing Mary, for whose family he works as a chauffeur, he begins to feel he has the power to retaliate against whites and to make them take him seriously. And after meeting Boris Max, his lawyer, Bigger finds, for the first time in his life, that he can release his feelings by talking about them, as well as by acting them out violently.

When reading *Native Son*, you will have to decide

whether Bigger is merely a passive product of his oppressive environment or whether he learns to assert himself meaningfully against that environment. Certainly Wright shows you conditions that may have made Bigger the surly, hostile person you see in the novel. Discriminatory housing practices force him to share a one-room apartment with his mother, brother, and sister, and he has little opportunity for employment. Possessing only an eighth-grade education, Bigger cannot compete, and he feels hopeless. That hopelessness can easily turn into anger in a city where the possibility of a better life dangles so tantalizingly before Bigger's eyes.

But you can also argue that Bigger learns to assert himself against this oppressive environment. The novel begins with an alarm clock waking Bigger. And throughout, Wright contrasts two conflicting tendencies of Bigger's. One is to fall back into sleepy passivity. The other is to awaken to the world around him, to stand up against it, and to chart his own course. This awakening begins when he kills Mary. Do you think Bigger can achieve a sense of self-worth only through brutality and violence? Do you think he ever wakes up, or is he living in a world of illusion throughout the novel?

How does Wright himself feel about Bigger? He certainly portrays Bigger's brutality in such gory detail that you may well feel that he is trying to turn you against Bigger. But by letting you know Bigger's state of mind, does he make you sympathize with Bigger anyhow? Some readers suggest that, while Bigger's violence is self-destructive, it is no more self-destructive than more passive responses to oppression. Through the character of

Boris Max, however, Wright appears to imply that political action would be a more constructive path. What do you think?

Bigger dominates the novel. He is a fully drawn individual, but you may also see him as a symbol or representative of something larger. Note the possible symbolism of Bigger Thomas's name: his first name suggests "big nigger," and the second may be an ironic reference to "Uncle Tom," a term for blacks who are eager to win white approval. At the very least, he may represent one rebellious black response to a racist society. Wright indicated that he modeled Bigger on a Bigger Thomas he knew as a child and on at least four other similar men he met later in life. The first Bigger terrorized Wright and his playmates, but Wright secretly admired him. Likewise, the other "Biggers" were also tough loners who defied both white society and the more passive blacks around them. But their rebellions ended in self-destruction.

Some readers see Bigger as a symbol of the predicament of all black Americans of Wright's time. Perhaps Wright encourages such an interpretation by calling Bigger a "native son." Even blacks who would never have considered acting like Bigger were products of the same society and may have felt the same feelings and faced the same choices. And you might even maintain that Bigger represents the plight of modern humanity, regardless of race. Isolated and misunderstood, Bigger must give his own life a value that none of society's institutions will give it. Note that Wright emphasizes Bigger's separation from black society almost as much as his antagonism toward whites.

Mrs. Thomas

Mrs. Thomas is a hard-working black woman who does all she can to keep her family together. Her main worry is her eldest son, Bigger. She thinks he's a troublemaker, doesn't like the gang he hangs out with, and wants him to get a job so her other two children can stay in school. Mrs. Thomas is also a religious woman who finds emotional support in prayer, and she fears that Bigger's rowdy life will lead to disaster.

Though Mrs. Thomas seems like a fine and decent person, by nagging Bigger to improve himself, she makes him angry. After Bigger kills Mary, he sees his mother as blindly and passively accepting the conditions of her life. This passivity enrages Bigger, and he feels humiliated when his mother begs the Daltons to help save him. Do you find his criticism of his mother justified? Is Mrs. Thomas's religion a source of strength or of weakness?

Bessie Mears

Bessie Mears is Bigger's girlfriend, who works long, hard hours, six and a half days a week, in the hot kitchen of a white woman's home. She finds relief at night by drinking. Although neither of them admits it to the other, Bigger and Bessie use each other. Bigger gives Bessie money to buy liquor, and in return she gives him sex. At times, however, Bessie seems to feel genuine affection for Bigger and to be emotionally dependent on him. She talks of marrying him, and, despite her fear and better judgment, she considers going ahead with Bigger's ransom scheme, if only to prevent him from walking out on her. Does she really care for him, or is this affectionate behavior just an act?

Bessie may represent one black response to an oppressive environment. You could view her drinking as a self-destructive reaction that does not challenge the conditions under which she lives. But Wright portrays Bessie sympathetically enough that you may see her as a victim. Note how Bigger uses her drinking to control her, forces her into his ransom plan, and when the plan fails, kills her. Do you sympathize with her plight, or do you identify more with the contempt her cowardice and passivity provoke in Bigger?

Mary Dalton

Though a millionaire heiress, Mary Dalton is a Communist sympathizer. A headstrong young woman, she defies her parents by dating a Communist. You don't get to know Mary well enough to decide whether her political convictions are solidly grounded or whether she simply enjoys the romance and excitement of a secret life with her radical boyfriend. She is likeable, though, and her desire to help blacks like Bigger is certainly sincere. But she is unaware of Bigger's feelings, and, despite her good intentions, she acts in a racist manner. She treats Bigger not as an individual whose friendship must be earned, but as a representative of the black race; and she seems to think her political views guarantee her the right to his companionship.

Because the character of Bigger Thomas is so central to *Native Son*, Mary is important mainly for her effect on Bigger. While she means only to help him, her whiteness and wealth make Bigger feel

self-conscious about his blackness and poverty, and
her treating him so familiarly confuses him, then
makes him feel ashamed at his confusion. From
that shame springs hate. In addition, Bigger knows
that white women are forbidden to black men and
that association with white women can invite ac-
cusations of rape. This potential danger makes
Mary's friendship even more threatening to Bigger. Though Bigger kills Mary accidentally, he
knows that he felt like murdering her anyhow.

Some readers think the white characters in *Native Son* are drawn less vividly than the black characters. Others suggest that such a discrepancy is
appropriate because Bigger, from whose point of
view the novel is written, would perceive the white
characters less clearly and more stereotypically than
he perceives the black characters. But Mary, who
arouses particularly strong feelings in Bigger, seems
more alive than some of the other white characters.

Jan Erlone

Jan Erlone, Mary Dalton's lover, is a Communist
thoroughly committed to the cause of racial justice
and social change. (Some readers think Jan was
modeled on Jan Wittenber, a white Communist ac-
quaintance of Wright's.) But Jan knows almost as
little as Mary about how black people think and
feel. You get the impression that he treats all blacks
alike rather than as individuals. As a result, Jan
makes Bigger ashamed and angry, although he is
trying only to treat Bigger as an equal. For example, he thinks that shaking Bigger's hand is a
friendly gesture, but Bigger finds such unaccus-

tomed familiarity from a white man confusing and suspects that Jan is mocking him.

Jan's attitude changes in the course of *Native Son*. When he visits Bigger in jail, he admits he was wrong to have expected Bigger to accept his offer of instant friendship. Jan even forgives Bigger for having killed Mary. Do you find Jan's forgiveness believable? Certainly, selfless people like Jan exist, but does Wright make this particular selfless character convincing? You might find Jan easier to accept if you saw him wrestling with his conflict about whether to forgive or to condemn the man who killed his girlfriend. But the novel's focus on Bigger and on Bigger's experience would have made such a portrayal difficult.

Boris Max

Boris Max is a lawyer who specializes in defending blacks, members of labor unions, Communists, and others he believes are victims of persecution and discrimination. He doesn't appear until the third part of *Native Son*, but there he becomes one of the novel's major characters. Max wants to help Bigger; he defends him in court and takes Bigger's case to the governor.

Max also befriends Bigger. Although he puts much more effort into his legal work for Bigger than into his human relationship with him, Max ultimately helps more as a friend than as a lawyer. Through talking to Max, Bigger seems to learn to define his own attitude toward his crime, even though that attitude shocks Max.

Max may not be a fully drawn human being, but he is an important vehicle for the statement of a political position. He believes that an oppressive society is responsible for Bigger's crimes and that, instead of lashing out blindly, Bigger should have united with others in political action demanding racial equality and social and economic justice. Max may be speaking for Richard Wright because at the time he wrote *Native Son*, Wright's political views were similar to those expressed by Max. While working on the novel, Wright told a friend that he needed the character of Max as a vehicle for his own ideas.

MINOR CHARACTERS

Buddy

Bigger's younger brother, Buddy, looks up to him and admires Bigger's toughness. But Buddy shows no signs of becoming as angry, aggressive, or rebellious as Bigger. To Buddy, Bigger's life seems exciting, but Buddy is not aware of how fearful and confused Bigger feels. After Bigger kills Mary, he sees Buddy's life as blind and meaningless.

Vera

Bigger's younger sister, Vera, is a gentle adolescent who wishes Bigger would stop causing so much trouble. She attends sewing classes, a sign of her desire to acquire a skill and to earn a living but also perhaps an indication of how limited her ambitions are. She obviously loves Bigger, but she feels he is mean to her. In particular, she objects to his looking at her. She thinks he stares at her, and his gaze upsets her and makes her self-conscious. Note that later in the novel, Bigger himself feels ashamed when Mary and Jan look at him. Like Bigger, too, Vera lives in fear, but while his response to fear is to strike out, hers is to shrink back. Wright establishes this difference in the opening scene: when a rat menaces the household, Bigger kills it, and Vera faints.

Reverend Hammond

Reverend Hammond is a black preacher and the spiritual guide of Bigger's mother. He appears briefly twice, when he visits Bigger in jail. Wright may be using Reverend Hammond to represent the black church. Hammond believes that the proper response to suffering is to turn to God and religion. When Jan urges that Bigger fight the fate that awaits him, Hammond opposes this course. In the end, Bigger angrily rejects Hammond's ideas. Do you find Hammond a sympathetic character? Is Wright criticizing the path that Hammond urges blacks to take?

Gus, Jack, and G.H.

Gus, Jack, and G.H. are Bigger's buddies and his partners in petty robberies. Like Bigger, they have no jobs and little prospect of bettering their lives. They shoot pool with Bigger, joke with him, and rob small black businesses. But they are not as daring as Bigger, for when he suggests robbing a white man, they hesitate. They seem more willing than Bigger to accept their limited lives. They also seem calmer and less intense. Bigger seems friendliest to Jack, but his relationship with Gus is the most complex. Despite their friendship, Bigger almost kills Gus in a fight. Gus seems to describe Bigger accurately when he says that Bigger's toughness is only a way of hiding his fear. Perhaps Bigger's anger at Gus is partly a result of Gus's accurate perception of him.

Doc

Doc runs the pool hall where Bigger and his gang hang out. He tolerates them even when they talk of robberies they want to commit and only intervenes when Bigger becomes violent.

Mr. and Mrs. Dalton

The Daltons are an elderly, rich white couple who sincerely desire to help blacks. Mr. Dalton donates money to put ping-pong tables into recreation centers for black youth. He hires young blacks like Bigger as chauffeurs. His wife encourages these employees to return to school and helps them to do so. But Mr. Dalton owns the real estate company that operates the building in which Bigger and his family rent a rat-infested room. His company charges blacks more than whites and does not allow blacks to rent in white neighborhoods. Thus, Mr. Dalton is partly responsible for the plight of Chicago's blacks. And despite their good intentions, neither Mr. nor Mrs. Dalton ever relates to Bigger as a human being. To them he is not an individual, but only one more poor black whom they are generously trying to help. Nor do the Daltons understand or sympathize with their daughter's radical politics.

Mrs. Dalton, who usually dresses in white, is blind. Her literal blindness may be symbolic of the blindness of all white people to the reality of black life. (The family name may refer to Daltonism, a form of color blindness.)

Peggy

Peggy is the Daltons' loyal Irish maid. She is kind to Bigger, but she identifies with the Dalton household rather than with her fellow servant, Bigger. When she speaks of the Dalton household, she uses the word "us," not "them." Like the Daltons, she sees Bigger as a timid black boy, no different from any other. She cannot imagine that he would have either the intelligence or the daring to commit a murder and to send a ransom note.

Britten

Britten is a private investigator employed by Mr. Dalton. Unlike Mr. Dalton, he is an overt racist. He doesn't think blacks are worth helping, is initially suspicious of Bigger, and calls him a Communist. But he doesn't believe that Bigger was able to commit the crime on his own, without Communist help. Thus, Britten's racism helps Bigger avoid detection.

Buckley

Buckley, the State's Attorney (prosecutor) of Illinois, is bent on advancing his own career by seeing Bigger condemned to the electric chair. When Bigger first sees Buckley's picture on a campaign poster calling for obedience to the law, he thinks of him as a hypocrite because he assumes that politicians are crooks. But Buckley does not appear in person until Bigger is in jail. Then Buckley tries to portray Bigger as a sex criminal, mass murderer, and Communist. He badgers Bigger into signing a confession and insists that he receive the death penalty. To Bigger, Buckley seems typical of the powerful whites bent on his destruction.

Other Elements

SETTING

One of the major themes of *Native Son* is the effect of people's environments on their behavior and personality. Thus, setting is especially important in the novel. The story takes place in Chicago in the late 1930s, when the United States had still not recovered from the Great Depression. Jobs are scarce, and Bigger and his pool-hall friends are among the many unemployed. Richard Wright was influenced by the literary school of naturalism, whose adherents tried to observe and record their world, and especially its more unpleasant parts, with scientific accuracy. Wright knew Depression-era Chicago well and drew heavily on his first-hand knowledge. In many respects, the Chicago of *Native Son* is an accurate representation even in its details. For example, Ernie's Kitchen Shack at Forty-seventh Street and Indiana Avenue was modeled on a real restaurant called The Chicken Shack, located at 4647 Indiana Avenue and owned by a man named Ernie.

Two aspects of Bigger's environment influence him especially strongly—his confinement to Chicago's black South Side ghetto and his glimpses of the dazzling white world, of which he feels he can never be part. Bigger's family shares a rat-infested room, but, when he sees an airplane flying overhead or views the glamorous life portrayed in a movie, he feels teased and tempted by a different, happier world. At the Daltons, Bigger is thrust directly into that freer, white society. The striking contrast between their impressive mansion and the

Thomases' one-room "kitchenette" apartment illustrates Bigger's frustrating predicament.

Many readers have pointed out, however, that the courtroom and jailhouse settings of Book Three are less realistic than the settings of Books One and Two, perhaps because Wright himself was less familiar with those environments. And, though few would contest that the hardships of life in Chicago's Black Belt were as oppressive as Wright portrayed them, some readers point out that the urban ghetto was also a place of opportunity for blacks by comparison to the Deep South, from which most of them had migrated. For example, in Chicago, Wright found the respect and encouragement that he had never experienced in rural Mississippi. But in *Native Son*, Wright doesn't seem to acknowledge that Chicago could hold out any hope at all for a poor black youth. Finally, many whites in Depression-era Chicago lived in poverty too, but because Bigger does not come into contact with them, they do not form part of this novel.

Despite their realism, the settings of *Native Son* also function symbolically. Wright's Chicago often has a nightmarish intensity in which external locations convey his characters' inner emotions. Bigger's confining apartment mirrors his feeling of being hemmed in in all other aspects of his life too. The rat that he pursues there foreshadows the hunted beast that Bigger himself will become. Likewise, the airplane Bigger sees overhead reminds you of all his frustrated aspirations to soar away from his limited life. At the Daltons', however, Bigger does not soar. Instead they consign him to the symbolic hell of their basement and its fiery furnace, an appropriate background for Big-

ger's swelling rage. And when Bigger flees the
Daltons', the snow of Chicago's wintry streets comes
to represent the white enemy that Bigger cannot
escape.

THEMES

The following are themes of *Native Son*.

Major Themes

1. RACISM

Native Son is an indictment of racism. Racism
affects Bigger's life at home, at the Daltons, and in
police custody. The Thomases must live in their
rat-infested apartment partly because no one will
rent to blacks in any other section of town. At the
same time, blacks are charged higher rents than
whites. When Bigger goes to the movies, one of
the films portrays blacks as jungle savages. After
his arrest, Bigger finds that the press and the public are using racial stereotypes to portray him as a
sex criminal and brutal mass murderer. And despite their best intentions, even the liberal Daltons
and the radical Jan and Mary act toward Bigger in
a racist manner by failing to recognize him as an
individual.

2. BLACK RAGE

Bigger Thomas is angry. You first see him in
conflict with his mother and sister. Later he turns
in fury on one of his best friends, Gus. Jan and
Mary also enrage him. He frequently thinks of
"blotting out" the people around him. And some
of his moments of greatest exhilaration occur when
he vents his hostility in violence.

Bigger's anger seems to be closely connected to his sense of racial identity. He is often furious at other blacks for their passive responses to the limitations placed on their lives by whites. And he is frequently enraged at whites for making him feel ashamed and self-conscious.

Does Wright share and approve of Bigger's fury, or does he present it as a tragedy? Your answer to this question will depend on whose views you think Wright shares. By narrating the novel from Bigger's point of view, Wright draws you into sympathy with Bigger. You can also argue, however, that Wright identifies more with Boris Max, who seems shocked and upset by Bigger's attitude toward violence. What is your response to Bigger's fury?

3. RELIGION

Although his mother is religious, Bigger decides that she is blind to the realities of her life. He sees his mother's need for religion as parallel to Bessie's for whiskey. Both, he thinks, are passive, escapist responses to racist conditions. At the end of the novel, Reverend Hammond tries to convince Bigger to pray. But Bigger appears to reject the black church, and presumably all religion, when he throws away the crucifix given him by Reverend Hammond. Bigger identifies the crucifix with the burning cross of the Ku Klux Klan.

Wright seems to be sharply critical of the black religious establishment and its representative, Reverend Hammond, who even objects to Jan's suggestion that Bigger try to fight back and save his life. You might argue, however, that Bigger's rejection of the cross and of religion is not neces-

sarily the author's rejection. Do you find the views
of either Reverend Hammond or Mrs. Thomas appealing? Or do you agree with Bigger's repudia-
tion of them?

4. COMMUNISM AND RADICAL POLITICAL IDEAS

Jan Erlone is a Communist, Mary Dalton is a
Communist sympathizer, and Boris Max is a lawyer who works closely with causes supported by
Communists. Even before any of these characters
appears in the novel, Bigger has seen a movie that
portrays a Communist as a maniacal bomb thrower.
Native Son contrasts the media image of Communists with Communist characters who are decent,
warm human beings. Some readers think Wright's
portrayal of his Communist characters is too ideal-
ized. On the other hand, Wright also shows that
neither Jan nor Mary understands Bigger and that,
despite their professed concern for black people,
neither can relate to a black man as an individual
human being. As a result, you might maintain that
the novel criticizes Communists even while portraying them as victims of unfair stereotyping.

In Book Three, Wright uses Boris Max to present
a radical social critique. Max argues before the judge
that Bigger's violence is a predictable response to
society's racism, which is the real criminal. Max
also tells Bigger that young unemployed blacks like
him should work with other blacks and with trade
unions and radical movements. Many readers think
that Max speaks for Wright and that Max's arguments are those of the Communist Party of Wright's
time. You might question whether Max ever really
understands Bigger, however. If you feel he doesn't,

this limitation might be evidence that he isn't a completely reliable spokesman for Wright. Do you agree with any of Max's arguments?

5. DETERMINISM AND FREEDOM

Bigger feels happier and freer after he kills Mary. His violence against a white woman gives him a sense of power. At the end of *Native Son*, he even implies that his killings expressed his deepest self. You could argue that through his violent rebellion, Bigger has transcended or risen above the passivity of the other black characters. From this point of view, Bigger's violence is an assertion of his freedom and a rebellion against society's constraints.

But Bigger's lawyer Boris Max suggests that Bigger is only a passive product of his society. Bigger's violence, he says, is a reflex created by the oppressive conditions of his life. From this viewpoint, Bigger is at least as blind, passive, and self-destructive as the novel's other black characters, and perhaps even more so.

Minor Themes

The relationship between *men and women* is another of the themes of *Native Son*. Bigger's affair with Bessie is affected by the difficult conditions of their lives. Each uses the other as a means of escape, but genuine love between them doesn't seem possible. Bigger is attracted to Mary, and she may be attracted to him, too, but the racial barrier prevents Mary from even understanding Bigger and makes Bigger fear and hate Mary. Another theme is Wright's critique of the *criminal justice system* in the U.S. Wright suggests that the court's verdict is predictable and perhaps even that the court is carrying out the will of the mob. *Alienation* (isolation) is an additonal theme of *Native Son*. Bigger is isolated from whites and blacks alike, and his acts of self-assertion cut him off from humanity even further. *Black family life* is another of the novel's concerns. Bigger's father was the victim of a Southern lynch mob. And Bigger's family lives in such crowded conditions that they get on each other's nerves. Finally the novel considers *media stereotyping*. Both the movies and the newspapers stereotype minorities, Communists, rich people, and criminals.

STYLE

Richard Wright favors short, simple, blunt sentences that help maintain the quick narrative pace of the novel, at least in the first two books. For example, consider the following passage: "He licked his lips; he was thirsty. He looked at his watch; it was ten past eight. He would go to the kitchen and get a drink of water and then drive the car out of the garage." Wright's imagery is often brutal and elemental, as in his frequently repeated references to fire and snow and Mary's bloody head.

Though the style is similar to that of much of the detective fiction of Wright's day, some readers find it perfectly suited to a novel told from the point of view of an uneducated youth, driven by overpowering feelings of fear, shame, and hate. Even the novel's clichés (stale or overused phrases or expressions like " . . . he had his destiny in his grasp") may fit a central character who gets his information about the larger world from the cliché-ridden mass media.

Wright worked within the literary tradition known as naturalism. The naturalists wanted to compile social data in such a way as to give a scientific explanation for their characters' behavior. But Wright goes beyond merely presenting social data. At times *Native Son* seems more like a nightmare than like social science. Note that Wright was also attracted to the horror and detective stories of Edgar Allan Poe.

One of Wright's stated goals was to make readers "feel" the heat of the Daltons' furnace and the cold of a Chicago winter. But he also makes the cold and heat symbols of the external forces aligned against Bigger and of the powerful emotions raging within him. Other patterns of imagery that appear throughout the novel include beasts (the rat, Bigger as a hunted animal, Bigger portrayed in the newspapers as a gorilla); suffocation (the fire being choked out by the accumulated ashes, Bigger's own feelings of suffocating confinement); blindness (Mrs. Dalton's literal blindness, the other characters' figurative blindness); staring (Bigger staring at Vera, Mary and Jan staring at Bigger, the cat staring at Bigger after the murder); walls (the wall of the Thomases' apartment and of Bigger's jail cell, the "looming white walls" of Jan and Mary in the car).

POINT OF VIEW

The third-person narrator of *Native Son* is neither objective nor omniscient (all-knowing). Almost throughout the novel, he sees through the eyes of Bigger Thomas. He is aware of Bigger's thoughts and feelings, but he sees other characters only from the outside. This point of view has several consequences. For example, some readers think the novel's white characters are less fully developed than the black characters. But they argue that this discrepancy stems from Bigger's greater understanding of his fellow blacks. Likewise, the novel uses stylistic clichés (stale or overused expressions like, ". . . he had his destiny in his grasp") that may be justified as being the terms in which Bigger understands his world. And, though some readers think that Jan would have been more believable if Wright had shown his internal conflicts, Wright could not have done so without abandoning the focus on Bigger.

Perhaps the major effect of narrating *Native Son* from Bigger's point of view is to allow you to sympathize with a character who might otherwise seem repugnant. You understand what Bigger is going through, even if no one else around him does. But you should not automatically assume that Bigger's outlook is that of Richard Wright. In fact, one of the major controversies about *Native Son* is whether Wright approved of Bigger or condemned him.

Wright is not completely consistent in his determination to adhere to Bigger's point of view. The greatest lapse is found in Book Three, where Wright presents all of Max's speech to the judge, even though he says that Bigger could only understand Max's tone of voice, not his words. And Wright occasionally uses more sophisticated words and phrases than Bigger would have been likely to use. For example, he has Bigger "looking wistfully upon the dark face of ancient waters upon which some spirit had breathed and created him."

FORM AND STRUCTURE

Native Son is divided into three books, titled "Fear," "Flight," and "Fate." The absence of chapter divisions or flashbacks helps maintain the novel's rapid narrative pace. It also emphasizes the turning points that occur at the end of each book. In each book, the circumstances of Bigger's life change, and in each book his attitude toward life changes too.

As its title suggests, Book One portrays a fearful Bigger. His fear leads him to three violent confrontations, each more consequential than the one before. After killing the rat, he leaves home for the pool hall, where he almost kills his friend Gus. The confrontation at the pool hall helps him decide to take the job at the Daltons. But the day ends in his murder of Mary Dalton. The murder of Mary is the climax of Book One. Bigger resolves the crisis created by Mary's death when he decides to burn her body and turn suspicion upon Jan.

In Book Two, Bigger's "Flight" has double meaning. At first the killing of Mary takes away his fear. He feels a sense of power and freedom that he has never felt before. Although he had wanted to fly as an aviator and thereby escape his confining life, killing Mary is as close as he has ever come to escaping. But the second part of Book Two sees him fleeing rather than flying. The book's climax is the discovery of Mary's bones. The crisis created by that discovery is resolved when Bigger falls from his rooftop perch and the police capture him.

The first two books are more similar to each other than either is to the third. While "Fear" and "Flight" focus on the gruesome events of a murder story, "Fate" emphasizes a combination of social analysis, philosophical and political argument, and Bigger's internal reflections. The first two books relate many dramatic events, but Book Three contains more talk and thought than external action. The climax of Book Three is the judge's rejection of Max's arguments and the death sentence he pronounces upon Bigger. Bigger must then decide how to approach his impending death. That decision is the final resolution of both Book Three and the novel as a whole.

The Story

BOOK ONE: FEAR

Though Wright uses no chapter divisions, he occasionally separates sections with a line of dots. This study guide follows Wright's divisions and gives each one a title to make the narration easier for you to follow.

BIGGER IN THE GHETTO

The first part of Book One introduces you to Bigger Thomas and to his family and friends. It portrays Bigger's fear, his desire to escape, and his violence.

* * *

Native Son begins with the sound of an alarm clock. Like much of the novel, this scene shows the realistic details of Bigger's life and environment. But it can be read symbolically too. The opening paragraphs depict Bigger's literal awakening in the morning, and your first glimpse of him is of a man hovering between sleep and wakefulness. Later you will learn that Bigger's life alternates between sleepy indifference and angry, often violent, activity. Many readers interpret Bigger's development of his own sense of self-worth as a movement toward greater awareness, a gradual awakening. According to this interpretation, the opening of *Native Son* both foreshadows Bigger's future (his eventual awakening) and illustrates his present emotional state (half-asleep, half-awake).

Bigger, his brother Buddy, his sister Vera, and his mother dress. The boys have to look away while the women dress; then the women look away while the brothers dress. The apartment contains only one room, and this scene illustrates the close quarters in which this family lives. But it also introduces the shame that results from being looked at. Later Bigger will burn with shame under the gaze of Mary and Jan. But the tiny family apartment makes being looked at an issue even at home.

Before they have finished dressing, the family notices a rat scurrying along the floor. Bigger orders Buddy to block off the rat's hole. Then he corners the rodent and kills it by beating its head in with a skillet.

NOTE: The rat scene   In the essay "How 'Bigger' was Born," Wright says that when he began writing *Native Son*, he could not think of an opening scene. He decided to proceed without one, and when he had almost finished the novel, this opening came to him. Note how much it accomplishes. Of course the rat illustrates the miserable conditions under which the Thomases live. But in addition, Bigger's killing the rat helps reveal his character: he enjoys the violent clash. The rat is the first of many animal images in this novel. And the fate of the cornered, hunted rat foreshadows Bigger's eventual fate, just as the crushing of its head foreshadows Bigger's murder of his girlfriend Bessie in Book Two.

Bigger teases his sister with the dead rat and makes her faint. His mother is upset, and she says that she sometimes regrets having given birth to Bigger. She calls him "black crazy." Bigger's relationship with both his mother and his sister seems quite tense. He feels that a wall separates him and his family. Over breakfast, Mrs. Thomas urges Bigger to take a job that he has been offered. If he refuses, the family will be removed from public assistance. Her nagging angers Bigger.

Bigger leaves the house and heads for the pool hall to visit with his friends, Jack, Gus, and G.H. He sees workers putting up a campaign poster for the State's Attorney, Buckley, who will be important in Book Three. Bigger thinks about a robbery he and his friends had once considered. Although they have held up some small black businesses in the past, this store is run by a white man named Blum. Robbing Blum's would be a big step for Bigger and his gang.

At the pool hall, Gus and Bigger stand outside and talk. They see a plane circling overhead. It is a skywriting plane, and the two young men watch the wispy white smoke gradually spell out the words, "Use Speed Gasoline," a message that only highlights the fact that neither Bigger nor Gus has any chance of owning a car. Like the opening scene in which Bigger kills the rat, this scene accomplishes several objectives. You learn that the black ghetto is not completely shut off from the outside white world, which intrudes teasingly, reminding Bigger and his friends of the possibilities denied them.

But the plane also becomes a symbol. It represents Bigger's desire to fly, not simply literally, by being an aviator, but also by soaring beyond all the limitations of his environment. Perhaps the airplane's white smoke adds to the symbolism by associating the freedom of flying with the color white. This scene ends with Bigger turning his fantasy of freedom into one of violence. He imagines using the plane to drop bombs on whites.

Gus and Bigger then play at being white. They pretend to be a general, a big businessman, and the president of the United States.

NOTE: J.P. Morgan   John Pierpont Morgan (1867–1943) was a financier and the son of John Pierpont Morgan (1837–1913), whose holdings he inherited. The Morgans had used their banks to gain control of a huge empire of industries, railroads, and insurance companies. They financed corporate mergers and in return gained major roles in the merged companies. One of the most important companies they controlled was U.S. Steel. Of course, the Morgans' economic power gave them tremendous political power as well. But to those who were opposed to such concentrations of wealth, the name Morgan became almost synonymous with what they saw as big business's excessive power.

Bigger and Gus continue to talk, and Bigger says that being black is "just like living in jail," an ironic statement in light of what eventually happens to him. Bigger feels that the white folks live in his stomach, where they burn like fire. Foreshadowing what is to come, he says that he expects that "something awful" will happen to him or that he will do "something he can't help." Gus understands, adding that the feeling is like one of falling. You may want to return to this conversation after you finish Books One and Two.

Bigger and Gus enter Doc's pool hall, where Jack and G.H. soon join them. Bigger reminds his three friends of their plan to rob Blum's, but the others are hesitant. Though Bigger taunts them for being scared, he is afraid too. Jack and G.H. agree to go along. As Bigger awaits Gus's decision, he begins to hate Gus because he knows that if Gus decides to go, the robbery will take place, and Bigger will have no excuse to back out. Finally, Gus accepts the plan, but he rightly accuses Bigger of being scared and of using his anger to disguise his fear. Bigger curses Gus, and the two almost fight. The four friends leave the pool hall and agree to return at three o'clock for the robbery.

Bigger realizes that he has emerged from his "curtain of indifference" and that he now feels an intense, violent energy. Note that he usually alternates between moods of indifference and violent anger. He seems to feel that viewing a movie will release some of the angry energy that has seized him.

Bigger and Jack go to a double feature. In the first movie, *The Gay Woman*, a rich young white woman meets secretly with her boyfriend, while her millionaire husband is busy at work. But one evening when the lovers are at a night club, a wild-looking man enters and throws a bomb at them. The boyfriend catches the bomb and throws it out the window before it can explode. It's revealed that the bomb-thrower was a Communist who thought he was attacking the millionaire husband.

Like the airplane trailing white smoke, the movie is another example of the way the white world teases Bigger and his friends with a dazzling freedom that they can never achieve. Because Bigger's new job will be at a white family's house, Bigger and Jack joke about the loose lives these whites seem to lead. During the next feature, a film about blacks dancing naked in the jungle, Bigger fantasizes about his new job at the Daltons'. Maybe Mr. Dalton will be a millionaire with a "hot" daughter who will want him to take her to the South Side. Maybe she'll have a secret boyfriend, and Bigger will drive her to see him.

NOTE: The South Side The South Side black ghetto of Wright's Chicago was a rectangle, one-and-one-half miles wide and seven miles long. Its western border was the tracks of the Central and Western Illinois Railroad, on the other side of which lived Mexican, Polish, and Irish immigrants. To the east was the University of Chicago and to the north a newly constructed white residential neighborhood. Though there were a few black enclaves outside the South Side and though the ghetto was gradually pushing further south, the South Side was almost a black city within the larger white city around it. It had some 200,000 residents, but just about the only jobs available within the ghetto's borders were for shopkeepers and gambling house owners.

When you finish Book One, you will see just how ironic this fantasy becomes. It comes true, but not in the pleasant way that Bigger hopes for. Note also that the movie presents the first Communist to appear in the novel. Bigger has no idea what a Communist is, and the movie portrays the Communist according to the popularly held image, or stereotype, of Communists, just as the other movie stereotypes blacks.

Thinking about the job at the Daltons' makes Bigger more uneasy than ever about the risk of robbing Blum's. When Bigger returns to the pool hall, Gus hasn't arrived yet, and when he finally does, Bigger, furious, picks a fight with him for being late. Gus runs off, and without him the robbery can't take place. On his way out, Bigger slashes Doc's pool table.

What does this incident tell you about Bigger? You've learned that he's afraid, that his fear turns easily into anger and violence, and that his violence turns more readily against other blacks than against whites. You may also have found him to be a loner, ill at ease with both his family and friends.

BIGGER AT THE DALTONS'

Bigger goes to the Daltons', where the unfamiliar surroundings intimidate him. He is excited about the new job, but he is extremely upset by the strange behavior of young Mary Dalton and her Communist boyfriend, Jan.

* * *

As the second half of Book One begins, Bigger is leaving for his job interview. He brings his knife and gun with him, as if only by being armed could he cope with the frightening power of the white world. When he reaches the high, iron fence of the Daltons' mansion, he is nervous. Bigger doesn't know whether to go in the front or the back, and, as he wanders around, he fears that if a policeman sees him, he may be accused of robbery or rape. After you read further, you may want to reflect on Bigger's fear of being accused of rape. However exaggerated such a worry seems at the moment, later you will see Bigger's fear come nightmarishly true.

Bigger goes through the Daltons' fence and thinks that even if he is doing wrong, the Daltons can only deny him the job, not kill him. This thought may also be ironic, in view of later events. Peggy, the Daltons' maid, lets Bigger into the house. Bigger is uncomfortable as he feels her staring at him. Everything about the house seems strange, and Bigger feels intimidated by the dim lighting, the unusual paintings on the walls, the quiet music playing, and the large, soft armchair in which Peggy has him wait. Soon, Peggy takes Bigger into Mr. Dalton's office.

Mr. Dalton speaks kindly but, like Peggy, he

gazes at Bigger, and his look makes Bigger feel self-conscious.

NOTE: Images related to the eyes and to sight pervade *Native Son*. Here, Peggy's "staring" and Mr. Dalton's "gazing" make Bigger angry and uncomfortable. Later, the way Mary and Jan look at Bigger will intensify those feelings. You should also note the guilt and fear Bigger experiences under the gaze of the Daltons' cat, and the shame Bigger's sister feels when he looks at her. Note, too, the emphasis put on blindness, both Mrs. Dalton's literal blindness and the symbolic blindness that Bigger discovers in his fellow blacks.

While Bigger and Mr. Dalton are talking, an elderly woman, Mrs. Dalton, enters the room. Her face and hair are so white that Bigger thinks she resembles a ghost. Later, she will also be dressed in white. Why do you think Wright emphasizes Mrs. Dalton's whiteness? Keep this emphasis on whiteness in mind, as it will become important later in Book One.

Though the Daltons are talking about him, Bigger cannot understand what they are saying. He feels as though there are hidden presences in the room; he feels blind. When Mrs. Dalton leaves, Mr. Dalton tells Bigger that she is blind. Bigger stands with his eyes lowered and shoulders stooped; he assumes that white people wish him to maintain this humble stance. Dalton asks Bigger for the note the welfare office gave him, and Bigger is so clumsy in trying to find it that he wishes he could wave his hand and "blot out" the man who is embarrassing him, or, failing that, blot out himself. Bigger's fear, shame, and self-consciousness as a poor black in a completely unfamiliar world of rich whites makes him feel humiliated. Regardless of your race or economic status, however, you can probably think of times when you have felt like Bigger feels during this interview.

Mr. Dalton tries to put Bigger at ease by saying that he was once a boy too, and he understands what Bigger is going through. You may take Mr. Dalton at his word, but you may instead think that he understands little indeed. Bigger's feelings do not derive from being a "boy"; rather they come from being poor and black. You may also want to question Mr. Dalton's calling twenty-year-old Bigger a "boy." Would Mr. Dalton have used this word to a white man the same age as Bigger? Could using a term traditionally applied by racists to black men show a lack of sensitivity on Dalton's part?

Then Mr. Dalton asks Bigger if he would steal on the job. The question appears to assume that Bigger would be naïve and stupid enough to answer "yes," if he in fact would steal. In his autobiography, *Black Boy*, Wright says he was once asked the same question by a racist Southerner.

Mr. Dalton hires Bigger as a chauffeur. He makes two comments that you may find ironic in view of later events. He says, "I don't think we'll have any trouble," and he tells Bigger to take Sunday mornings off "unless something unexpected happens."

Before Bigger and Mr. Dalton are finished, Mary Dalton comes into the room. She asks Bigger if he is a union member, and she calls her father a "capitalist." Bigger, who knows little about unions and who doesn't know what a capitalist is, finds Mary's behavior upsetting.

NOTE: Bigger finds that Mary is not what he imagined her to be when he was watching the movie, *The Gay Woman. Native Son* frequently contrasts media images of the world with the realities these images distort. Bigger did not notice that one of the two movies he saw presented a false picture of blacks. And he believed the other movie's portrayal of both Communists and rich people. Wright will later show that the movie's depiction of Communists was false. But here he shows that the movie was unfair to rich people too. Keep this point in mind when you try to decide whether Wright was excessively influenced by radical political doctrine.

Bigger also has no idea what Mr. Dalton is talking about when he says that he supports the National Association for the Advancement of Colored People (NAACP).

NOTE: NAACP The black intellectual W.E.B. Du Bois and a group of white progressives founded the NAACP in 1909. Its goal was complete racial equality, at that time a radical cause supported by few mainstream political leaders, black or white. By Richard Wright's time, the NAACP had become a moderate civil rights organization with strong roots in the black middle class and clergy. Wright strongly disliked the NAACP's refusal to support the more militant protest tactics of the Communist

Party. But in 1941, the NAACP gave him its high-
est award, the Spingarn Medal, for *Uncle Tom's
Children* and *Native Son*.

Peggy brings Bigger into the kitchen and gives
him food. She comments that Mr. Dalton gives
money to "colored" schools, and she mentions that,
though his wife had millions when he married her,
he also made a great deal of money in real estate
after the marriage. You have already been told that
Mr. Dalton may be the owner of the real estate
company that rents the Thomases their apartment.
Do you find it ironic that a man makes money rent-
ing blacks rat-infested apartments and then donates some of that money to black schools? Do
these donations make you think better of him or
worse? Peggy says that she understands "colored
people." You will have to decide later whether she
understands Bigger any better than Mr. Dalton does.
Does she assume that all blacks are alike?

Peggy shows Bigger the basement furnace he
will be in charge of stoking. Then she takes him
to his room, which is decorated with the previous
chauffeur's pictures of black boxers and white female movie stars. Wright's use of white stereotypes of blacks has sparked controversy. One such
stereotype is that black men are especially attracted to white women and vice versa. Wright
seems to be suggesting that Bigger's predecessor,
Green, was fascinated by white women. Do you
think he is suggesting this? Some readers have criticized Wright for seeming to affirm racist stereotypes. Do you agree or disagree with this criticism?

Bigger feels enthusiastic about his job. His first

assignment is to drive Mary to her university class.
But on the way there, Mary orders Bigger to change
directions. She does not plan to go to her class at
all and wants Bigger to keep her true destination
a secret. You may find Mary quite appealing. But
note how she orders Bigger around. Though she
seems to be trying to treat him as an equal, she
doesn't hesitate to order him to light her cigarette,
for example.

Bigger has mixed feelings about Mary. Like all
rich whites, she scares him, and her unpredicta-
bility makes her seem even more dangerous. But
she treats him as a human being and thus gives
him an unfamiliar feeling of freedom. Bigger is even
more confused when they pick up Mary's Communist boyfriend, Jan. Jan and Mary violate the
unspoken rules that, in Bigger's experience, have
always governed black-white social contact. Jan
insists on shaking hands with Bigger, and he wants
Bigger to call him Jan instead of "sir." Jan insists
on driving the car himself, and he has Bigger sit
between him and Mary. Then both Jan and Mary
demand that Bigger take them to a restaurant in
the black ghetto. They make Bigger feel even worse
by asking him to eat with them.

Bigger thinks Mary is laughing at his confusion.
He feels self-conscious and ashamed, and then angry as a result. He believes people are looking at
him, and he wishes he could take a heavy object
and "blot out" the car with the three of them in it.

Do Jan and Mary deserve Bigger's hate? They
are the first white people to treat him as an equal,
and you may well regard Bigger's feelings toward
them as a tragic misunderstanding. But you could
also argue that Jan and Mary do act in a racist
manner toward Bigger. According to this line of

thought, they tell him what to do without considering his feelings, and instead of trying to win his trust, they simply order him to be their friend. Is their insisting that he take them to his neighborhood a sign of friendship or of arrogance?

Perhaps some sign of racism is also implicit in their frequent references to Negro spirituals, one of which Mary even sings in black dialect. Had they gotten to know Bigger as an individual, they might have found that, while his mother sings spirituals, Bigger has no use for them. They offer Bigger fried chicken. Later, driving back from the restaurant, they compliment blacks on having so much "emotion," another stereotype. You may also want to refer to this section of the novel when considering whether Wright was uncritical of Communists. Do Jan and Mary behave like people capable of uniting blacks and whites in a political struggle for social change?

At the restaurant, Mary, Jan, and Bigger drink beer and rum. The three continue drinking as Bigger drives Mary and Jan around the park. By the time Jan gets out to catch his streetcar, Mary is extremely drunk. Bigger has to carry her to her room, and, as he does, he worries about what the Daltons would think if they found him with their drunken daughter in his arms. But Bigger also feels excited by the physical contact with Mary. He has never been so close to a white woman. As he carries her into her bedroom, he begins to kiss and caress her. Then he sees a white blur in the doorway. It is Mrs. Dalton.

NOTE: Wright emphasizes that Mrs. Dalton appears to Bigger as a "white blur." Earlier, he described Mary and Jan as two "looming white walls." Is Wright suggesting that to Bigger the whiteness of these people is more important than their characteristics as individuals? On one level, Bigger may see the advancing figure of Mrs. Dalton as the impending vengeance of the white world for his having come close to violating one of the major taboos of white society.

Bigger feels as though he is falling from a great height. He is terrified. Although Mrs. Dalton cannot see, she can hear. As she enters the room, he holds a pillow over Mary's head to prevent her from speaking. When Mrs. Dalton leaves the room, Bigger realizes that Mary is dead. He has suffocated her.

NOTE: Sexual imagery and violence A scene that began with a sexual encounter has ended in violence, not love. Nonetheless, the language may suggest sexuality. While suffocating under the pillow, Mary's body "surges" toward Bigger. Her "body heaves" with increasing intensity as she digs her fingernails into his arms. Finally, she sighs, and her body relaxes. Some readers have found sexual imagery in the next scene, in which Bigger burns Mary's body on what Wright refers to several times as the "red bed of coals." Though Bigger has killed only by accident, you could argue that Wright is deliberately conjuring up the feared image of sexual violence committed by black men against white women.

Bigger now has to figure out how to cover up what he has done. He remembers that Mary had been planning to go to Detroit the next morning. He puts her body in her trunk and carries it to the basement. Then he decides to burn the corpse in the furnace. The head will not fit, however, so he cuts it off. First he tries gently with a knife, then he uses a hatchet. He sees Kate, the Daltons' white cat, watching him and almost decides to burn Kate too. When Mary's body is finally burning in the furnace, Bigger decides to turn suspicion toward Jan. After all, Jan is a Communist, and people will be ready to believe him capable of any evil.

Why does Wright make this scene so gruesome? Bigger himself thinks of the incident as "unreal, like a nightmare." Though from the rest of Book One you can consider Bigger an innocent victim of racism and bad luck, this scene may make you see him as the villain of a gory horror story, perhaps one in the tradition of Edgar Allan Poe, one of Wright's favorite writers. Some readers think Wright revels in creating a scene that could be a white racist's worst nightmare. What do you think?

BOOK TWO: FLIGHT

FROM MARY'S DEATH TO BESSIE'S DEATH

In this part of Book Two, Bigger finds that having killed Mary makes him feel freer than ever before. Acting with a new sense of power, Bigger sends the Daltons a ransom note in which he claims

that Mary has been kidnapped. But Bigger's plans
go awry, and he flees with Bessie, whom he kills.

* * *

As Book Two begins, Bigger is waking up on
Sunday morning. Wright says that he wakes "like
an electric switch being clicked on," perhaps foreshadowing Bigger's death in the electric chair. He
is back in his family's one-room apartment. Compare this opening to the start of Book One. Once
more, you see Bigger struggling between sleep and
wakefulness, then bickering with his family. But
this morning is different from the previous one.
The first difference is Bigger's fearful memory that
he has killed Mary, cut her head off, and burned
her body. He must protect himself. He throws his
bloody knife and Mary's purse into a garbage can
outside.

Over breakfast, however, Bigger's attitude
changes dramatically. At the beginning of Book
One, he was afraid. Now his fear is gone. Though
he had killed Mary by accident, he no longer thinks
of her death as an accident. After all, he had felt
like killing many times before. Now that he has
actually killed, he feels proud and fulfilled because
he has been more daring than anyone would have
believed possible. He looks at his family and their
apartment as if seeing them for the first time. Scan-
ning his brother, mother, and sister, he compares
them to whites he has seen. The Thomases now
appear to him as blind creatures of habit, incapable
of bold actions. But he also realizes that the Daltons, too, are blind; after all, they had underesti-
mated him. Remember that Bigger had felt ashamed
when the Daltons and Jan looked at him. Now he
shames each member of his family with his own
unrelenting stare.

NOTE: James Baldwin's critique   Some readers
have criticized Richard Wright's portrayal of the
black community. Probably the most famous attack came from the novelist and essayist James
Baldwin. Himself an important black writer influenced and helped by Wright, Baldwin claimed that
"Bigger has no discernible relationship . . . to his
own people," that by comparison to Bigger himself, the blacks around him would have been "far
richer and far more subtle and accurate illustra-
tions of black life," and that the "shared [black]
experience which creates a way of life" is missing
in Wright's work. Baldwin's criticisms have sparked
much controversy. Do you think that Wright necessarily shares Bigger's negative impression of his
fellow blacks?

As Bigger leaves for work, his brother Buddy
confronts him. Bigger had taken Mary's money from
her purse, but in his hurry, he has accidentally
dropped it on the floor. Buddy hands the money
back to Bigger and asks him if anything is wrong.
For a moment Bigger even thinks of killing his little
brother but then decides to trust that Buddy won't
tell anyone about the money.

Before returning to the Daltons', Bigger stops to
see his old gang. He feels like a man who has
awakened after a long illness. He treats Gus, Jack,
and G.H. kindly because he no longer fears them.
As he continues to the Daltons', Bigger realizes
that he has always looked at whites as "a great
natural force," a threatening one, like a storm. Remember this metaphor during the blizzard that begins later in this section. Bigger wonders if blacks

could ever get together and stand up against whites. He thinks maybe they could unite if they had a ruler to tell them what to do. He's heard good things about the German dictator Adolf Hitler and the Italian dictator Benito Mussolini. Perhaps some day the blacks will have such a leader, he thinks.

NOTE: Shortly after the publication of *Native Son*, Richard Wright wrote an essay in which he said that Bigger Thomas could easily have become either a Communist or a Fascist. And he claimed that his research into the rise of Nazism in Germany helped him in his formulation of Bigger's personality. In "How 'Bigger' was Born," Wright says that both Fascists and Communists recruit from the "dispossessed and disinherited" of "a dislocated society." From what you know of Bigger up to this point, do you think he would be a potential recruit to any mass movement? What evidence can you offer in support of your opinion?

Throughout much of this section, Bigger's thoughts travel in two different directions. On the one hand, he feels free and powerful, and he sees his killing of Mary as a "supreme and meaningful act." On the other hand, his mind keeps returning guiltily to images like Mary's bloody head and the outstretched arms of her blind mother. Readers have interpreted Bigger's personality in several different ways. Some focus on the degree to which he is a victim. After all, the killing was an accident, and afterward he was only trying to protect himself. Others emphasize the ways in which Bigger may be a heroic rebel. At this point in the novel, this image seems to be developing into Bigger's self-image, and he certainly makes you aware of his justified anger toward whites. Still other readers see Bigger as cold and brutal. Which interpretation do you favor? What evidence do you have for your opinion?

Wright may have deliberately created a character who would evoke conflicting emotions. He doesn't let you slip into easy pity (Bigger, after all, is proud of what he has done) or easy identification (Bigger, after all, keeps reminding you of the horror of his actions) or easy condemnation (Bigger, after all, had little choice in what he did).

Back at the Daltons', Bigger finds the household increasingly worried about Mary. First, Peggy notices that the car was left out all night. Then, when Bigger pretends to be ready to drive Mary to the train station for her trip to Detroit, Peggy and Mrs. Dalton are surprised to find that Mary is not home. They assume that she left for Detroit early, and they send Bigger to the station with her trunk. But Mrs. Dalton feels around in Mary's room and notices that Mary has left some of her traveling clothes behind. She decides to question Bigger, but she is hesitant to push her interrogation too far, apparently because, as a rich white, she would be embarrassed to let a poor black servant know anything is wrong. Note how the subtle racism of Bigger's well-meaning employers helps him avoid detection.

Bigger decides to visit his girlfriend, Bessie. On his way there, he wishes he had gotten more money from killing Mary and resolves that "next time" he will do better. He wants to brag about his crime to the white faces around him, but he knows he can't. So he wishes that "he could be an idea in their minds." He wants a picture of the killing and the burning of Mary to hover before their eyes.

NOTE: "Bigger Thomas . . . in [the] skull" This comment of Bigger's may suggest something about Wright as well. In one of his critical essays on Wright, James Baldwin said, "No American Negro exists who does not have his private Bigger Thomas living in his skull." Some readers believe that Wright's purpose in writing *Native Son* was to make the Bigger Thomas in his own skull "an idea" in the "minds" of whites. In other words, he wanted to hold before whites an image of the black rage they refused to acknowledge, just as Bigger wants to hold before whites an image of the bold actions they would never expect from him. Remember that before Wright, even much black American literature portrayed Afro-Americans as the good-humored, gentle people many whites wanted them to be.

Bigger arrives at Bessie's. She is upset and jealous that he has been away so long, but when he shows her the roll of money that he took from Mary's purse, she warms up to him. They make love, and afterward she mentions that the Daltons live in the same section of town as the murderers Loeb and Leopold. She reminds him that Loeb and Leopold killed a boy and then tried to get ransom money by pretending that the boy had been kidnapped.

Your Comments, Please.

We are delighted that you have selected BARRON'S BOOK NOTES to assist you in your literature studies. This card is being provided so that you may assist us in our continuing effort to make our Book Notes the finest available. Your comments and suggestions will be sincerely appreciated. Just drop the completed card in the nearest mailbox — the postage is paid.

Thank you for your assistance.

1. **Title of Book Note you read** _____

_____

2. **Were you pleased with the book?** ☐ Yes ☐ No

3. **Was there any aspect of the book you particularly liked?** ____

_____

4. **Particularly disliked?** _____

_____

5. **Would you recommend this book to your friends?**

   ☐ Yes ☐ No Why? _____

_____

6. **Have you ever used any other book notes?** ☐ Yes ☐ No

   Which one? _____

7. **How would you rate BARRON'S BOOK NOTES as compared to the other series?** ☐ Much Better ☐ Somewhat Better
   ☐ About the Same ☐ Not as Good

8. **Any suggestions for improvement?** _____

_____

9. **Are there any other titles you would like to see added to the series?** (please list) _____

_____

Name _____

Address _____

City _____ State _____ Zip _____

School name, grad. year _____

_____

BUSINESS REPLY CARD

FIRST CLASS   PERMIT NO. 14   WOODBURY, NEW YORK

POSTAGE WILL BE PAID BY:

BARRON'S EDUCATIONAL SERIES, INC.

113 Crossways Park Drive

Woodbury, NY 11797

Bessie has given Bigger the idea that he can do what Loeb and Leopold did. He wonders if he can use Bessie in his plot and hopes she will act with him "blindly." Bigger thinks that Bessie, like his family, is blind. She works long hours in a white woman's kitchen, then sleeps with him because he will buy her liquor. Bigger wants Bessie to collect the ransom money from the Daltons. He doesn't tell her that he killed Mary but says that Mary has eloped with Jan. Bessie is afraid to participate in this plot, but Bigger insists. He gives her the money he took from Mary's purse.

You may see Bessie as a passive woman who uses whiskey as an escape, and you could argue that all she wants from Bigger is money. Some readers have suggested that Wright is especially critical of his female characters. They point to Mrs. Thomas's religious escapism and Mary's naïveté. But you may also feel that Wright paints Bessie's plight quite sympathetically. And Bigger's calculating coldness toward her may increase your sympathy. Perhaps Wright felt compassion for both Bigger and Bessie without feeling that either responded correctly to the oppressive conditions of their lives. If Bigger hadn't committed his crime, would his relationship with Bessie have been able to blossom?

NOTE: Bessie feels quite free to steal from her white employers. But Bigger's ransom scheme frightens her. If you read *Black Boy*, you will notice that Wright claims that Southern whites didn't mind their black employees stealing from them. A little petty theft enabled the whites to confirm their stereotypes of blacks and to justify their racist attitudes, Wright says. Perhaps Wright had this thought in mind in contrasting Bigger and Bessie. Bessie's small crimes don't challenge or defy the whites the way Bigger's offenses do.

As Bigger heads back to the Daltons', he is confident. At last his life has a purpose. The Daltons have found that Mary never arrived in Detroit. Mr. and Mrs. Dalton question Bigger, and he tells them that he left Jan and Mary together last night. The Daltons now suspect Jan of having played a role in Mary's disappearance.

A little later, Bigger is in the basement looking at the furnace. Mr. Dalton enters with a private investigator, Britten. Britten is a hard, cold man, and Bigger feels his hostility. The investigator questions Bigger closely, and Bigger now reveals that Mary did not go to her class. Bigger tells the truth about the evening except when he says that Jan and Mary came home together and that Jan had told him to leave the car outside and to take the trunk downstairs. Then Britten flusters Bigger by accusing him of being a Communist. Though Britten is an overt racist, both he and Mr. Dalton finally agree that Bigger is being honest.

While napping, Bigger has a dream. He is carrying a heavy package. When he opens it, he discovers that it is his own bloody head.

NOTE: Bigger kills the rat by crushing its head, and he cuts off Mary's head. Later, you will see him batter Bessie's head as well. Does this dream suggest that Bigger's assaults are really directed at the psychic demons that inhabit his own head? Remember that his violence has often been a way of coping with his own hate, fear, and shame. The dream may suggest that, despite his violence, Bigger's head (and the feelings within it) are still a heavy burden to him.

Bigger is awakened for another confrontation with Britten and Mr. Dalton, who now have Jan with them. Bigger maintains his lies even in Jan's presence.

Afterward, Bigger thinks about clearing the accumulated ashes out of the furnace. But he is afraid to do so for fear of finding pieces of Mary among them.

Bigger goes outside, and Jan confronts him in the street. Bigger refuses to talk to Jan and pulls a gun on him. Jan is making Bigger feel quite guilty.

Now Bigger looks for an abandoned building to use as a drop-off point for the ransom money. He finds one and returns to Bessie's where he writes a ransom note, which he signs with the word "red" and decorates with a hammer and sickle, the Communist emblem. Bessie is extremely upset. She accuses Bigger of killing Mary, and he confesses. Now that Bessie knows about Mary's death, Bigger thinks of killing Bessie to keep her quiet. He threatens Bessie until she tearfully agrees to go along with his plans.

As Bigger works out his ransom plan, Wright supplies you with some broader social background. You learn that Mr. Dalton's real estate company rents apartments to blacks only in the most run-down area of the city. And you learn that when blacks first moved into that neighborhood, whites tried to chase them away by bombing their houses. Now whites have fled the neighborhood, and many of the buildings are abandoned. Note how *Native Son* mixes sociological description, a psychological portrait of Bigger's inner conflicts, and dreamlike symbolism. Look for all three, and see how well Wright blends them into a unified whole.

Bigger returns to the Daltons' and excitedly slips the ransom note under the door. His dinner is waiting for him in the kitchen, but despite all his bold crimes, he hesitates to eat without permission. The old, timid Bigger seems to coexist with the braver new one. When Mr. Dalton receives the ransom note, the family panics. Britten returns and questions Peggy. She says Bigger is " 'just like all the other colored boys.' " You could argue that Wright is continuing to expose his white characters' racism. If you take this line of thought, you could contrast Britten's blatant racism with Peggy's unconscious prejudice. Remember also that the racial stereotypes held by whites are helping Bigger turn suspicion away from himself. No one seems to believe that a black could have either the intelligence or the boldness to carry out such a crime.

Now Bigger is no longer alone in his basement furnace room. Britten and his men set up their headquarters there, and the press soon arrives as well. Bigger is aware that, while everyone is talking about Mary, her body is burning in the fiery furnace right next to them. He thinks events resemble a "tortured dream." Mr. Dalton reads the ransom note to the excited newspapermen. The Daltons' cat jumps on Bigger's shoulder, and the photographers snap a picture.

NOTE: Wright was an admirer of the American poet and storywriter Edgar Allan Poe (1809–1849). In one of Poe's stories, "The Black Cat," a cat becomes a symbol of a murderer's guilt. Wright uses a similar device here. Bigger often feels that the Daltons' cat is looking at him accusingly. In an appropriate twist, Wright makes the cat white instead of black. Some readers also see the Daltons' cat as a parallel to the rat in the Thomases' apartment. Bigger hunts and kills the rat but thinks that the cat is helping hunt him.

Bigger reads a newspaper. The story about the Daltons has a strongly anti-Communist tone. Remember the distortions in the movies that Bigger saw in Book One. Now, in Book Two, Wright seems to portray similar distortions in the press. He continues with this theme as the reporters question Bigger and try to slant their story so it portrays a "primitive Negro who doesn't want to be disturbed by white civilization." The reporters also look for anti-foreign, anti-Semitic, and anti-Communist angles.

Meanwhile, the fire in the furnace is dying because Bigger has not cleaned out the ashes. Peggy asks him to clean them out, but he is afraid Mary's remains will appear in front of Britten and the reporters. Instead of cleaning the ashes, which are blocking the fire's air supply, Bigger simply adds more coal. The stifling fire begins to smoke, choking everyone. One of the reporters grabs Bigger's shovel and cleans out the ashes. He notices that they contain some of Mary's bones and an earring.

The smoke clears, but Bigger's fear has returned, and it is choking him. He goes to his room and jumps from the window to the snow below. Bigger's effort at liberation seems to have failed.

You may now find the title of Book Two ironic. In Book One, Bigger wanted to fly. In Book Two, his killing of Mary gave him the feeling of freedom that he had previously associated with flying. But now he may be worse off than before killing Mary. He is now in flight in a different sense; he is fleeing. Do you think Wright is showing the futility of Bigger's violence here? Or has Bigger gained some personal strength from his violence?

NOTE: **Fire and snow**   Throughout Book Two, Bigger has been walking back and forth between the cold and snow of the blizzard and the heat of the basement with its burning furnace. Some readers think the icy, white blizzard represents the white world that Bigger has always seen as a natural force. If so, it adds an element of irony and fatalism, for its cold surrounds Bigger even while he is confidently planning his ransom scheme. Some readers also feel the furnace represents the fires raging within Bigger. Shortly after the fire chokes on its ashes, Bigger chokes on his own fear. Some readers point to the fire and the snow as evidence that Wright's main purpose in writing *Native Son* was not to present a realistic social analysis but to create a symbolic tale with a dreamlike atmosphere. Do you think he could be doing both?

Bigger heads for Bessie's. He reads the newspapers, which have reported the ransom note. For the first time, he tells Bessie the details of Mary's death. She says he will be accused of rape, and he believes she is right. But he also thinks he has committed rape many times in his mind, not just against white women but against all whites. Rape, he thinks, is what one does when backed into a corner and forced to strike out.

Bessie is distraught, and Bigger tells her that they will have to flee together. They hide in an abandoned building, where Bigger has sex with Bessie despite her protests. He is afraid she will give him away to the police, so, when she is asleep, he kills her by beating her head in with a brick. Then he dumps her body down an air shaft. Later, he realizes his money was in her dress.

You may have noticed how Bessie's murder seems to replay Mary's death, but much more brutally. In both cases, Bigger and his victim have been drinking, but Mary plied Bigger with liquor in fun, whereas now Bigger bitterly forces Bessie to drink. In both cases, some sexual contact precedes the killing, but in the second instance the sexual encounter is rape. And, of course, Bessie's death is premeditated, not accidental. Have Bigger's recent experiences made him more brutal? Regardless, the differences between these two acts of violence further heighten the contrast between the glamorous world of rich whites like the Daltons and the harsh world of the black ghetto. Note that despite all his fantasies about striking out at whites Bigger's most brutal act is against a black.

As Bigger tries to sleep, he reflects on what has happened. In reading this passage, try to form some judgment about Bigger's character. He feels that his murders have been the most meaningful actions of his life because he has finally acted on the hatred he has always felt. So despite the failure of Bigger's ransom scheme, you have evidence here that his acts of violence have given him a new sense of self-respect. On the other hand, some readers use this same reasoning of Bigger's to condemn him for not feeling sufficient remorse for his crimes. Bigger's reverie continues: He condemns his mother for using religion as an escape, and he condemns Bessie for escaping with whiskey. But then Bigger has what seems to be a new thought. He wishes he could merge with the rest of humanity and not be set apart from others just for being black. His earlier fantasies were of a purely solitary liberation. Where does this new aspiration come from? Could it be a result of his experiences of the last two days?

BIGGER'S FLIGHT AND CAPTURE

Bigger flees eight thousand armed men pursuing him. He is finally captured.

* * *

Bigger steals a newspaper and hides in another abandoned building. The news story about him assumes he was a rapist. It describes the reaction of the white community to his crime: whites are attacking blacks on the street, smashing the windows of their homes, and firing them from their jobs. One news item particularly galls Bigger. The police assume that Jan had something to do with the crime because they cannot believe a black could have done it by himself. Bigger also discovers that the police are searching the South Side door to door. They are closing in on him.

Bigger is extremely cold and hungry.

NOTE: Wright's description of Bigger's hunger may strike you as especially vivid. Remember that Wright knew hunger first-hand as a child and rarely had enough to eat.

Bigger looks into an apartment. He sees a couple making love with their three children watching and remembers similar childhood experiences in his own one-room apartment. He is aware of the contrast between the large, empty abandoned buildings and the one-room apartments in which black families are forced to live. In this section, Wright provides ample evidence both for those who see *Native Son* as primarily sociological, a protest against unjust conditions, and for those who view it as primarily psychological, a portrait of a man fighting back against impossible odds. Bigger thinks about the scarcity of apartments in the Black Belt, a scarcity created by the confinement of blacks to one small neighborhood and by the frequent condemnation of buildings within that area. He also thinks about rents for blacks being higher than rents for whites, about businesses in black neighborhoods being owned by whites, and about the prices being higher than those of businesses in white sections of the city. How much has changed since Wright's time?

While Wright fills in the details of the racist social context that produced Bigger, he also keeps returning to Bigger's personal struggle. Bigger debates whether he should give up or keep fighting. You might see this conflict as a new level of Bigger's perpetual struggle between sleepy indifference and angry tension. Wright contrasts Bigger's attitude to that of other blacks. Bigger overhears two black men arguing. One blames the Bigger Thomases of the black community for the fact that whites mistreat blacks. The other says that whites will hate blacks no matter what. Blacks should fight back and stand up for Bigger Thomas, he says. Even within the world of the novel, Bigger Thomas is becoming a symbol of something larger than himself.

Bigger falls asleep and awakens to hear a church congregation singing. Despite finding religion tempting, he refuses to accept it. He finds an empty apartment in which to hide. A newspaper reports that eight thousand armed men are closing in on him, and when he hears them arrive at his building, he climbs to the roof. They find him there, and he flees. As Bigger realizes that he will be captured, he begins to retreat behind his "wall" or "curtain" of indifference. He hides on top of a water tank, but they wash him down with a fire hose. As Bigger falls, remember Gus's description of his feeling of falling. Also look back on Bigger's fall from the Daltons' window. Bigger wanted to fly, but his attempt ends in a fall, a fall foreshadowed early in the novel. The police drag Bigger by the feet with his head banging along the ground. Remember Bigger's violence against heads (the rat's, Mary's, and Bessie's) and his dream about his own bloody head. The police stretch Bigger out as if to crucify him. He loses consciousness.

NOTE: Symbolism For a novel that uses much socially accurate detail, *Native Son* also employs many recurring symbols. For example, as the white mob closes in on Bigger, the color white seems to appear everywhere—in the white snow, the white map, the white milk Bigger imagines, the "white heat" the newspapers speak of. Animal imagery also abounds in this urban jungle: Bigger envies the rat he sees; one black man says that his people are all "dogs" to whites; at one point, Bigger is "on all fours." The whites who seemed to Bigger like a natural force use rushing water to capture him. The water, which comes from a fire hose, douses Bigger, a man who has felt a fire in his stomach and whose emotional state has already been compared to a furnace.

BOOK THREE: FATE
BIGGER'S JAILHOUSE VISITS

Many people visit Bigger in jail. Bigger signs a confession.

* * *

Bigger has been in a stupor. He refuses to eat, talk, or move. Like the first two books, this one begins with Bigger struggling between sleep and wakefulness, but this struggle is more profound.

Bigger seems to be on the verge of giving up entirely, but he still has a spark of hope. He wishes he could find a new way of living. Taken to the inquest into Mary's death, he sees many faces looking at him from the audience. Thinking they are making sport of him, he feels as though he is falling; then he faints.

Bigger wakes up back in his cell and asks for a newspaper. The story in the paper is violently racist, referring to Bigger as a beast incapable of fitting into civilization.

NOTE: Robert Nixon   This newspaper story is so extreme that you may think Wright was exaggerating. In fact, the story is an only slightly fictionalized adaptation of a piece that appeared in the Chicago *Tribune* on June 5, 1938. When Wright was about halfway finished with his first draft of *Native Son*, a young black man named Robert Nixon was accused of raping a white woman and beating her to death with a brick. He was convicted and executed in the electric chair. Wright used many details of the Nixon case in his novel, and this racist news story was among them. Here is one more instance of Wright's use of realistic detail.

Now a series of visitors enter Bigger's cell. Some readers think Book Three centers on whether Bigger will be executed. Others feel the major conflict of the book is not about what will happen to Bigger but about what attitude he will take toward a fate that seems certain. If you agree with the second view, you may think that the people who visit Bigger are in a sense struggling for his soul.

One of the major protagonists in the struggle enters first. Reverend Hammond is Mrs. Thomas's preacher, and he urges Bigger to turn to Jesus. Bigger hates Hammond's religious message because it makes him feel as guilty as does the hatred of the whites. In this regard, do you think there is irony in Hammond's talk about washing Bigger's sins as "white as snow"? Remember how snow has already come to represent the hateful power of the whites.

Then Jan comes in. He says that he had been blind before, that he had wanted to kill Bigger for a while, but that he now understands Bigger's hatred and wants to help him. Jan urges Bigger to defend himself in court. He has a major effect on Bigger, and Wright expresses this effect with the same images he has used before in the novel. Bigger feels as though "someone had performed an operation on his eyes"; he feels as though a "curtain" has been opened; he feels as though a rock has detached itself from the "looming mountain of white hate." Jan urges Bigger to believe in himself and reminds Bigger that he believed enough to kill. Jan brings a lawyer named Boris Max. But perhaps even more important than Jan's offer of legal defense is his penetration of Bigger's wall of isolation.

The State's Attorney, Buckley, enters next. If Hammond's message is to turn to religion and Jan's is to fight back, then Buckley's seems to be to give up. He tells Bigger that they already have enough evidence to convict him, so he may as well confess.

The Daltons arrive, followed by Bigger's friends

and family. Bigger is aware of his family's shame under the eyes of the white people, and he again is proud of his murder, which, he feels, has washed away his shame. With his family around him, Bigger believes for the first time that he has not been alone, that his family is part of him. To make his mother happy, Bigger agrees to pray. All the visitors leave except Buckley.

Bigger has experienced many different emotions in this section. But two may be especially significant. At times, he seems to want to trust other people, including some white people. At other times, he seems to want to return to his proud isolation and anger. Which of these two attitudes do you think Wright approves of? Some readers think his political views suggest the former. What evidence can you draw from the novel to support your interpretation?

Buckley asks Bigger to confess to many rapes and murders and to implicate Jan in his crimes. Bigger is so discouraged and so in need of someone to talk to that he confesses to what he has done, but not to the other things Buckley asks him to confess to.

THE INQUEST

The Daltons and Jan are interrogated at an inquest. Later, Bigger sees a burning Ku Klux Klan cross and rejects the cross Reverend Hammond had given him.

* * *

Bigger lies crying on the floor of his cell. Why, he asks, is he not able to communicate his feelings to others?

Then Bigger is handcuffed and brought back to the inquest. A spectator hits him in the head.

NOTE: In the Nixon case, the bereaved husband of the murdered woman attacked the handcuffed defendant at the inquest. Later in this section, Bigger is brought to the Dalton house and photographed baring his teeth. Wright also based that incident on the Nixon case.

Mrs. Dalton is the first witness. The coroner's questioning of her is fairly routine, but he becomes hostile when interrogating Jan. He asks Jan several times if he is a foreigner. Presumably he thinks Jan will be easier to portray as sinister if he is seen as a foreigner. Then he asks questions that suggest that Jan had presented Mary as a sexual gift to the "drunken Negro," Bigger. The coroner further insinuates that Mary was used as bait to encourage Bigger to join the Communist Party, and he uses Jan's friendly behavior toward Bigger as evidence of Jan's evil qualities. Bigger sees that Jan, like himself, is an object of hate.

Next Mr. Dalton is called, and Boris Max questions him about his real estate business. Max points out that Dalton restricts blacks to one part of the city and charges them higher rents than he charges whites. Some readers have found Max's behavior unlikely. They wonder whether such sharp interrogation of an old man whose daughter has just been murdered could possibly win a jury's sympathy. Do you agree with this critique?

When Mr. Dalton leaves the stand, the coroner brings in his next piece of evidence—Bessie's body. Bigger realizes that no one cares about his having killed a black woman. They are just using Bessie's body to inflame opinion against him and to convict him for having killed a white woman. The white people are still abusing Bessie, just as they did when she was alive.

Bigger is formally indicted for murder.

Many readers question the need for this section. They claim it repeats information already presented, doesn't advance the plot very far, and, except during the questioning of Jan, doesn't change Bigger's feelings. But other readers point out that in this section Wright's attack on racism, including the racism of the judicial system, becomes substantially more detailed. Some readers feel Wright has already made that case quite well earlier. However, because he focused so heavily on the horrors of Bigger's crimes in the first two books, he may now need to remind readers of the horrors of the society that Bigger thought he was attacking. How much do you think this section accomplishes?

The police take Bigger back to the Dalton house. They demand that he reenact the rape and murder. He refuses. As they return Bigger to jail, a would-be lynch mob has gathered. Bigger sees a burning cross, the emblem of the Ku Klux Klan. He associates it with the cross the Reverend Hammond had given him in his cell. In anger, he throws the Reverend's cross away and refuses to let Hammond visit him again.

BIGGER TALKS TO MAX

Max interviews Bigger. For the first time, Bigger puts his deepest feelings into words.

* * *

As he sits in jail, Bigger notices that even there blacks and whites are segregated. Wright seems to be continuing his indictment of racism and of the criminal justice system. One prisoner refers to Bigger as the guy "they got for that Dalton job." Even among his fellow criminals, Bigger seems unlikely to find understanding. Then a stranger is dragged into Bigger's cell. He is foaming at the mouth and screaming that someone has taken his papers. Another prisoner tells Bigger that the newcomer went insane from studying too much. The maniac claims that someone stole a book he wrote and that the book explained the racist conditions under which blacks live.

You may find this brief incident rather odd. Some readers feel the man is a middle-class parallel to Bigger in that the only way he can protest racism is to go wild and crazy. And people notice only his craziness, not his message.

After the strange prisoner is removed from Bigger's cell, Max enters.

NOTE: In the real-life Nixon case, the defendant was initially represented by the International Labor Defense (ILD), on which Max's organization, the Labor Defenders, appears to have been modeled. But the ILD's role was small, and the National Negro Congress soon replaced it. Wright has deliberately magnified the role of white radicals

here. The bulk of Nixon's support came from the
leaders of Chicago's black community. This change
may have enabled Wright to emphasize his radical
political views. But it also helped him explore Bigger's changing attitudes toward whites.

Max encourages Bigger not to give up. He points
out that the same people who hate blacks also hate
unions, Communists, and Jews. Then he asks Bigger more about his crimes, and Bigger finds that
he wants to communicate his reasons for killing.
He tells Max that he hated Mary, and while talking
about Mary, whose looking at him made him feel
shame, he remembers how his younger sister Vera
had felt ashamed when he looked at her. Saying
that he wanted to rape Mary because white men
blame such behavior on blacks whether they commit it or not, Bigger tells Max more about his feelings of unhappiness and hatred, and Max expresses surprise that Bigger never trusted black
leaders and that he had no interest in voting.

The feelings Bigger expresses to Max are ones
you have been aware of all along. But this moment
is the first time Bigger has *spoken* of these feelings
to anyone. After Max leaves, Bigger imagines a
world divided into tiny isolated cells. He wonders
what would happen if people reached out of their
cells and touched each other. Would there be electricity between them? Bigger wishes he could live
to find out. Ironically, he will be killed by the quite
different electricity of the electric chair.

Many readers have sensed a conflict between
the message that seems to be emerging from Book
Three and the impact of the first two books of the
novel. Book Three appears to be developing an

appeal for interracial cooperation. Most of the first two Books pointed up the unlikeliness of such cooperation, given the depths of both white racism and black anger. Some readers reconcile the two points of view by suggesting that Wright uses the character of Bigger to warn whites about what will happen if social conditions do not change. Other readers think the impact of Bigger's character is so strong that the appeal for interracial solidarity seems sentimental by comparison. Do you think the balance between the two messages would be different if Wright were completing *Native Son* today?

NOTE: Through much of American history since the Civil War, two competing political tendencies have vied for the loyalty of blacks. One calls for blacks to gain access to housing, schools, jobs, and other American social and political institutions. People advocating these goals usually want blacks and whites to work together in achieving black integration into American society. The other tendency calls for blacks to gain control over their own housing, schools, jobs and other separate black social and political institutions. Advocates of these goals often want blacks to organize separately from whites. Certainly the views of Max and Jan emphasize the former opinion. And at this point in the novel, Bigger himself is moving in that direction. Some readers, however, have seen a separatist thrust in much of *Native Son*, especially where it emphasizes the depth of the gap between the races. Do you feel the novel emphasizes one perspective over the other?

BIGGER'S TRIAL

Max enters a guilty plea for Bigger and requests a sentence of life imprisonment. He blames Bigger's crime on oppressive social conditions. The judge sentences Bigger to death.

* * *

As he awaits trial, Bigger wishes he could again hide behind his curtain of indifference, but he no longer can. He realizes that two battles are raging, Max's battle in the courtroom and his own inner struggle over his attitude toward life and death.

Bigger's trial begins. The spectators are shocked when Max enters a guilty plea. Max has decided that a jury will be too biased. He will argue before the judge that Bigger should receive life imprisonment. Buckley, the prosecutor, fears that Max will try to prove that Bigger is insane. Thus, Buckley calls sixty witnesses to testify to Bigger's sanity.

The next day the defense presents its case. Bigger arrives in the courtroom before Max, and his brief wait makes him realize how dependent he has become on Max.

NOTE: The famous lawyer Clarence Darrow (1857–1938) was attorney for the defense in the Leopold-Loeb case. As you already know, the Leopold-Loeb murder was Bigger's inspiration for sending the Daltons a ransom note. Wright later told friends that he used Darrow's plea in that case for some of the material in Max's speech to the judge.

In his plea to the judge, Max speaks of the public

hostility to Bigger. Then he reviews the history of slavery and of black oppression. He emphasizes that he does not want to evoke sympathy for Bigger and that he does not see him as a victim, a point to remember in deciding whether you consider Bigger a victim. Max issues a warning: Bigger is the product of black oppression, and killing him will only produce new Biggers and more black violence. Given the conditions under which he lived, Bigger's crime was "instinctive," Max says, adding that Bigger's psychology is "the psychology of the Negro people." Then he discusses Bigger in more detail. For Bigger, he says, killing was an "act of creation" and Bigger's attitude is itself a crime. But this attitude is a product of white civilization. Love is impossible for a man like Bigger, says Max, and he concludes with the specter of millions of Biggers rising up against their white oppressors. Max urges the judge to send Bigger to prison, where he could begin his life anew.

Max's speech raises several questions. Given its repetition of much that has gone before, why did Wright include it at such length? Is it a credible speech for an attorney to use in defense of such a client? Does it represent the interpretation of Bigger Thomas conveyed by the novel as a whole? What is your opinion?

You may wonder whether such a controversial plea would be the best way to save a client from the electric chair. But other considerations may have been more important to Wright than credibility. Some readers feel that having presented the murders exclusively from Bigger's point of view, Wright needed to go outside Bigger to clarify his own attitude toward his major character. Though Mary's killing may have been instinctive, after the killing, Bigger felt that he was taking charge of his own destiny. So Max's interpretation of Bigger's behavior is not exactly the same as Bigger's interpretation of his own behavior. But if Wright agrees with Max that Bigger is merely a passive product of his environment and that Bigger is representative of all blacks, then why has he made Bigger behave so differently from the novel's other black characters?

Buckley sums up the prosecution's case. He says that the main crime was rape, and he calls for the death penalty. The judge recesses the court for an hour and returns with a sentence of death.

BIGGER'S FINAL TALK WITH MAX

Bigger and Max talk once more. Max encourages Bigger to believe in himself, and Bigger responds by affirming the value of his killings.

* * *

Bigger wishes that he could mingle with others and break out of his isolation before he dies. A white priest had visited him recently, and he had thrown coffee in the cleric's face. From that action, Bigger gained the same satisfaction as from his talk with Max. Apparently his old angry pride and his new desire to communicate coexist within him.

Max sends Bigger a telegram. The governor has rejected Bigger's plea for clemency. Bigger must die. Shortly thereafter, Max visits Bigger for the last time.

Max tries to comfort Bigger in the face of death, but instead of being comforted, Bigger wants to communicate his feelings to Max, and he wants

Max to help him resolve his conflicts. He reminds Max of the night they spoke and says that Max had helped him see himself and others more truly. He wonders if the people sending him to the electric chair might have much the same feelings he has.

Max replies by talking about the people who own property and control society. They have the same feelings as the rest of us, he says, but they make themselves believe that others, like blacks and workers, are not human. On both sides, people are fighting for their lives, but only one side will win. He urges Bigger to believe in himself, for those who believe in themselves can contribute to the social struggle.

Max and Bigger don't seem to understand all of what the other is saying. Bigger doesn't appear to grasp Max's concept of a society divided into two contending classes—workers and capitalists. But Bigger responds to Max's call for him to believe in himself. Believing in himself does not necessarily mean believing in what Max wants, however. Bigger reaffirms himself by reaffirming the value of his killings. What Bigger says makes Max afraid and upset, but Bigger now feels "all right." As Max leaves, Bigger tells him to say hello to Jan, the man who had once made Bigger feel shame and hatred. Now Bigger calls Jan by his first name, just as Jan had once asked him to. Apparently, Bigger has found his own way toward contact with others.

Why didn't Wright let Max and Bigger come to complete agreement? Some readers feel that Wright was sympathetic to Max's position but that he wanted a realistic conclusion. Perhaps he did not think that a conclusion in which an alienated black youth was readily converted to a socialist view of politics would be believable, either in light of the novel itself or of the political conditions of Wright's time.

On the other hand, like Jan earlier in the novel, Max may not have been able to see Bigger as an individual. He thinks that blacks, as a group, should behave in a certain way, that they should be activists. Max wants Bigger to believe in himself, but Max thinks he knows what form Bigger's self-affirmation should take. You may have occasionally had people advise you to stand up for yourself but not like it when you stand up against them. To be true to *himself*, Bigger may have to take a different path from the one Max has marked out. At the end, Bigger affirms himself by refusing to repudiate his violence. But he also learns to reach out to others for the first time. Is Wright suggesting that given existing social conditions, violence was the only way Bigger could be true to himself? Or is he implying that if people like Max and Jan had approached him earlier, he might have taken a different course?

A STEP BEYOND

Test and Answers

TEST

1. The reporters ask Bigger   _____
   - I. if he likes eating with white people
   - II. what he thinks of private property
   - III. whether he has seen any suspicious people around
   - A. I and II only   B. I and III only
   - C. I, II, and III

2. Bigger throws away his cross when he   _____
   - A. sees an emblem of the Ku Klux Klan
   - B. becomes a Muslim
   - C. is told to by the Communists

3. In Bigger's first meeting with Mr. Dalton,   _____
   Dalton asks him
   - A. how many jobs he has held
   - B. whether he will steal if hired
   - C. what his politics are

4. Bigger fails to clean the ashes from the   _____
   furnace because he is
   - A. forgetful
   - B. protesting menial work
   - C. afraid of seeing Mary's remains

5. Max questions Mr. Dalton about his   _____
   company's policy of

     I. charging blacks higher rents than
       whites
    II. refusing to rent apartments to blacks
       outside the South Side ghetto
   III. refusing to hire blacks for
       management positions
   A. II and III only   B. I and II only
   C. I, II, and III

6. Jan and Mary ask Bigger to take them to   _____
   A. a black night club   B. his home
   C. a restaurant in his part of town

7. Bigger kills Bessie because he   _____
   A. is jealous
   B. is afraid that she will turn him in
   C. has developed a taste for killing

8. In Bigger's final conversation with Max,   _____
   he says,
     I. "But what I killed for, I *am*!"
    II. "Tell Jan hello."
   III. "I want to live."
   A. I and III only   B. I and II only
   C. I, II, and III

9. Bigger's mother is   _____
   A. religious   B. politically active
   C. frequently drunk

10. Bigger's sister doesn't like Bigger's   _____
   A. taking a job outside the home
   B. looking at her   C. killing rats

11. What is *Native Son*'s attitude toward religion?

12. Does *Native Son* endorse violence? Explain.

13. Is *Native Son* a novel of social realism, or is it a dreamlike, symbolic tale? Back up your answer with evidence from the novel.

14. How convincing are the characters of Jan and Max?

15. What social institutions does Richard Wright criticize in *Native Son*?

ANSWERS

1. A   2. A   3. B   4. C   5. B   6. C
7. B   8. B   9. A   10. B

11. If you wish to emphasize Wright's critique of religion, you can point to Bigger's comparison of his mother's religion to Bessie's alcohol. Bigger comes to see religion, like whiskey, as an escapist response to victimization. Note that Reverend Hammond, a representative of religious sentiments, even objects when Jan urges Bigger to try to save his life. And Bigger's rejection of Reverend Hammond's cross seems to be a step toward his self-affirmation at the novel's end.

But you do not necessarily have to assume that Bigger's views are those of the author. Mrs. Thomas is a decent woman who tries hard to keep her family together. And Reverend Hammond shows no signs of being vicious or intolerant. You may want to claim that Max, rather than Bigger, speaks for the novel as a whole. In this way you could argue that the novel neither indicts nor endorses religion, but merely presents it as a fact of black community life.

12. You may want to point out the ways in which Wright emphasizes the horrors of violence. If he wanted to endorse violence, why would he dwell on images of Mary's decapitation, for example? The only deliberate act of vio-

lence is the killing of Bessie, and Wright shows this act to have been both brutal and futile. Mary's death was an accident, and it leads to Bigger's capture and execution. Moreover, Max, who may be speaking for Wright, sees Bigger's violence as a product of society's violence but not as a morally justifiable act.

On the other hand, Bigger affirms his killings at the end of the novel. And the killings seem to have been part of a process that finally enables him to reach out to Max and Jan. You can point to the way in which Wright shows Bigger gaining a new self-confidence, a sense of freedom, and insight into the world in the wake of his killing Mary. While you may not be able to argue convincingly that the novel actually endorses violence, you can make a case that it doesn't condemn violence in circumstances such as Bigger's.

13. You can maintain that the principal concern of *Native Son* is to portray the oppressiveness of society's institutions in a convincingly realistic manner. For example, use the section of Book Two in which Bigger is fleeing the police. In the midst of this desperate human drama, Wright finds ways of describing Chicago's discriminatory housing practices and other social abuses. Bessie's character allows him to portray the effects of low-paid domestic work. Book Three presents an even more detailed attack on racism in Max's questions and speeches.

But you can use much of the novel's imagery to argue that Wright is creating an intense nightmare, a fantasy of black rage and vengeance. His emphasis on the fiery heat of the furnace, his use of the symbolic blizzard, and his creation of the white cat as a guilt symbol are devices you can point to if you want to make a case that social realism is not the novel's main purpose.

14. To argue that Max and Jan are not convincing characters, emphasize their implausibly perfect goodness. For example, you can point to Jan's ready willingness to forgive the brutal murderer of his girlfriend and even to find him a lawyer. Max barely seems to exist outside the courtroom. Moreover, you can claim that his courtroom speeches are not the ones a lawyer defending his client would be likely to make. Why would he berate the aging father of a murdered daughter? This behavior is better explained by the fact that Wright created Max as a spokesman for his political and social views.

On the other hand, you may want to point to Jan's behavior with Bigger and Mary as evidence that he is not perfect at all. Following this reasoning, you can argue that Wright makes Jan a fairly complex personality whose unconsciously racist conduct undermines his good intentions. And you can excuse Jan's change of heart at the end by saying that it would have seemed much more plausible if Wright had been able to depart from Bigger's point of view and show readers Jan's internal struggle. As for Max, you can point to his confusion during his final conversation with Bigger as evidence that he too is imperfect and not merely a spokesman for Wright's politics. You can also claim that his courtroom argument becomes more plausible when one realizes that Max is making it to a judge and not to a more emotionally impressionable jury.

15. Among the institutions discussed in *Native Son* you may want to mention are the press, the cinema, the courts, the electoral system, the real estate industry, the church, boys' clubs, the small white businesses that operate in the black ghetto, and the system of charity. For Wright's critique of the press, examine the reporters who gather at the Daltons' in Book Two and the newspaper accounts of Bigger's case in Books Two and Three. Wright criticizes the cinema in his description of the grossly distorted films Bigger and Jack see in Book One. Book Three portrays a judicial system that seems to have condemned Bigger to death from the start. Note especially the coroner's behavior at the inquest and the judge's refusal to deliberate for more than an hour. The ability of a liar and hypocrite like Buckley to get elected may be an implicit critique of the electoral system. Wright criticizes Mr. Dalton and his real estate practices, most pointedly in the inquest scene of Book Three. Dalton's practice of giving charity to boys' clubs while forcing blacks to pay higher rents than whites seems to indict the philanthropy of rich whites. And Bigger mentions that his gang planned their robberies at the boys' clubs. During his flight, Bigger observes that businesses in the ghetto always charge more than those in white neighborhoods. Finally, reread the answer to question 11, for evidence of Wright's critique of religion.

Black Boy

THE AUTOBIOGRAPHY

Black Boy: A Record of Childhood and Youth is Richard Wright's autobiographical account of his life beginning with his earliest memories and ending with his departure for the North at age nineteen. In *Black Boy*, Wright tells of an unsettled family life that takes him from Natchez, Mississippi, to Memphis, Tennessee, back to Jackson, Mississippi, then to Arkansas, back again to Mississippi, and finally to Memphis once more, where he prepares for his eventual migration to Chicago.

Most readers agree that *Black Boy* is a highly selective account, more selective than the term "record" in its subtitle suggests. At the time Wright wrote *Black Boy*, he was already an accomplished author of fiction. He had published a collection of short stories called *Uncle Tom's Children* and the highly successful novel *Native Son*. Wright chose carefully the experiences he includes in *Black Boy*, the ones he highlights, and the tone in which he writes about them. Many readers even think that he invents some of the incidents. Most agree ever, that Wright crafts his autobiography for the precise impact he wants.

The Characters

Of course, the central character of *Black Boy* is young Richard Wright. To distinguish between this young character and the author looking back on him many years later and even occasionally inventing incidents about him, this guide follows the standard practice of referring to the former as "Richard" and the latter as "Wright." Wright presents Richard as a rebellious youth. Usually hungry and malnourished, he loves to retreat into the imaginary world of the novels he reads. Richard refuses to accept the strict religion of his grandmother and even rejects his mother's more moderate religious faith. As he gets older, he also stands up to the discipline his aunts and uncles impose on him and threatens to retaliate with physical violence. Later, the feisty, independent spirit Richard develops at home leads him to refuse to accept the codes of behavior the white world has set for Southern blacks. And when Richard finally decides to become a writer, that career represents a declaration of independence from those in the black community who ridiculed his ambitions and a declaration of war on the white racists who have oppressed him.

In the early chapters of *Black Boy*, the other important characters are the members of Richard's family. Richard's female relatives are more signif-
~ant in his life than the males. His mother often

disciplines him harshly, but the discipline clearly stems from her love. Abandoned by her husband and unable to establish economic independence from her strict mother, she suffers greatly. Her misery is increased by a stroke that ruins her health. Young Richard misses her during her illness and is deeply moved by her pain.

Richard gets along well with his Aunt Maggie, who, like his mother, is trying hard not to be dependent on Richard's grandmother. But he clashes angrily with his Aunt Addie, a strict Sunday School instructor who is determined to break Richard's independent spirit. He also has a difficult relationship with Granny, a deeply religious woman who seems to be genuinely worried about the state of Richard's soul. She is always ready to aid a family member in need, and she takes in Richard and his mother during Mrs. Wright's illness. But her conception of Richard's welfare does not consider his happiness an important issue. Much of Richard's rebellious spirit seems to develop from his struggle against Granny's rules.

On the other hand, Richard's father is important primarily for abandoning him and his mother and thus causing much of their deprivation. He seems to be a simple and somewhat selfish man with little interest in the effect of his behavior on his family. Three uncles also play a role in young Richard's life. Uncle Hoskins is a successful businessman willing to defy the whites who threaten him. He is generous with Richard and his mother, and his violent death is Richard's first brutal lesson in racism. Uncle Clark is another of the more prosperous members of the family. While he is quite willing to help Richard by feeding, clothing, and housing him, he is cool and unaffectionate and shows no understanding of Richard's fears and emotional needs. Uncle Tom, though, is one of the less successful uncles. Forced by his difficult financial situation to return to Granny's, Tom's insistence on becoming a disciplinarian to Richard seems to stem from his own sense of failure and humiliation. Richard's younger brother, Leon, doesn't seem very important in Richard's life. He doesn't share Richard's rebellious spirit and goes to live with Aunt Maggie after Mrs. Wright's illness.

Later in *Black Boy*, several other characters become significant. The principal of Richard's school tries to force Richard to abandon a speech the young man has written himself and to read the principal's speech instead. The principal sees himself as a successful black man who is only trying to help Richard escape the poverty to which he seems destined. But Richard considers the principal a failure because he does not challenge the codes of behavior that whites have set for blacks. Pease and Reynolds are two white optical workers who are quite friendly to Richard as long as he keeps his place and shows no interest in bettering himself. But they respond with vicious terror when he shows some interest in learning their skills. Shorty is an intelligent black worker who is willing to play the clown for the entertainment of whites. He thinks he is putting something over on the whites by making them believe he is a buffoon, and he is proud of his ability to get the whites to give him money. At times, however, he reveals his discouragement with the undignified way he is forced to live.

Other Elements

THEMES

1. RACISM

Black Boy attacks the racism of the South during the period Wright was growing up there (1908–1927). Many of the hardships of Wright's family life are direct or indirect results of racial discrimination. Once Wright enters the world of work, he finds racism pervasive and intolerable. The book concludes with Wright's fleeing the South and the racist conditions he has been forced to endure there.

2. DEVELOPMENT OF A WRITER

Many readers think the central focus of Wright's story is on his development into an artist and intellectual. From this perspective, the book is about the influences that shape Wright's desire to be a writer, the experiences that mold his creative outlook, and the obstacles he must overcome to escape the limited environment in which he is growing up. These readers feel that many of Wright's hardships are those of any sensitive and rebellious individual in a world that doesn't respect those qualities. They see the novel's conclusion less as a flight from racism and more as a move toward a new career and identity as a writer. Which of these two major themes do you think is more central? Or are they given equal weight?

Other Themes

Black Boy portrays the *deprivation* Wright faces growing up. It shows poverty, hunger, lack of emotional support, miserable living conditions, and Richard's response to these difficulties. The book also considers *family life*. For Richard, home is a place of intense emotional conflict, and his family forces him to fight back constantly in order to be able to pursue his own path. But the family also offers support in times of crisis, for example, when his mother has a stroke. *Black Boy* also considers Richard's *rebellion*. Richard's relatives criticize him for not conforming to their standards of proper behavior. Later, some of his friends criticize him for not acting as whites expect him to. But Richard defies all of them and continues on his rebellious course. Another theme is *religion*. Richard sees religion as meaningless at best and oppressive at worst. But he also finds some religious stories and imagery appealing. Wright also comments on the *emotional life of Southern blacks*. He is critical of the black community for what he sees as its emotional and cultural bleakness. But he also blames much of this bleakness on racism. *Black Boy* considers the theme of *isolation* too. Wright is often alone, and his loneliness is a source of both strength and unhappiness. Finally, *Black Boy* looks at the differences between *urban and rural life*. For Wright, the move to the city is liberating, but he seems to look back on country life with some nostalgia too.

ADDITIONAL CONSIDERATIONS

Black Boy is structured around the education of its central character. It's not a random or a comprehensive record of events. Wright chooses his incidents and structures his autobiography in such a way as to emphasize the gradual progress of

Richard's journey toward self-awareness and knowledge of the world around him. Narrated in the first person, the book usually adheres to the point of view of young Richard but occasionally changes to that of the mature author who comments on his past with the knowledge he has gained in the intervening years. Of his style in *Black Boy*, Wright later said that he wanted to make the reader "forget words and be conscious only of his response," that he even wanted to make words "disappear." In *Black Boy* Wright seems to be striving to state facts as plainly as possible. Do you think he succeeds? Do you find this goal desireable? Does Wright ever lapse from this goal?

The setting of *Black Boy* is particularly important. Though the book moves from one Southern city to another, from the Deep South to Memphis, Tennessee, and from almost all-black communities to workplaces dominated by whites, it is entirely set in the South. Wright had originally wanted the book to describe his life in Chicago as well, but his publisher decided only to accept the Southern portion. As a result, the book becomes in part an indictment of the South and of its oppressiveness toward blacks. How different do you think the impact of the book would have been if it had included a discussion of Wright's life in Chicago?

The Autobiography

CHAPTER I

The opening chapter recounts Wright's early childhood in Natchez, Mississippi, and his family's move to Memphis. It describes his early rebellion against parental authority, his poverty and hunger, and his unsupervised life on the streets while his mother is at work.

* * *

Richard is looking out the window and fretting about his mother's order to keep quiet. When he shouts with joy at a bird outside, she comes in and scolds him. Next he invents a game. He throws the straws of a broom into the fireplace and watches them burn, then holds some of the straws to the white curtains at the window. To his shock, the house is soon on fire. Afraid of punishment, Richard hides under the burning house. His parents, grandmother, and brother escape unharmed. When they find him, his mother beats him almost to death. He is sick for days thereafter and hallucinates about white bags, like the full udders of cows, dripping horrible liquid on him.

In this first incident Wright introduces many of the themes of *Black Boy* and some that appear in his fictional work as well. In his novel *Native Son*, published five years before *Black Boy*, the central character Bigger Thomas stands outside a pool hall and sees in an airplane flying overhead a symbol of the freedom that white society denies him. Here, young Richard also yearns for freedom and sees it in the flight of a bird. But for four-year-old Richard, the source of deprivation is family, not white society, as it is for Bigger. Note, though, the possible racial symbolism of the white curtains. Richard responds to his deprivation in a way that you will see is typical for him: through a rebellion that characteristically results in punishment. Finally, note the central role Richard's mother plays in this incident. Through most of the book, she remains the most important person in his life. Could the poisonous udders suggest a mother turned punishingly angry?

Wright remembers the pleasures of rural life. Then he describes his family's move to Memphis.

NOTE: Natchez and Memphis Natchez, Mississippi, was a city of twelve thousand when Wright lived there. Wright had been born in Roxie, a village with a population of two hundred, where his father worked on a farm. Wright's memories of rural pleasures may come from the time he spent in the Mississippi River port city of Natchez or from Roxie, where he lived until he was three. In any case, the transition to Memphis, an industrial center of one hundred thousand, was dramatic. Writing from the point of view of his childhood self, Wright does not tell you the reason for this move. The reason was that his father was unable to find steady work in Natchez, where economic deprivation forced the family to live with Wright's maternal grandparents.

Richard rebels again, this time against his father. He resents that man and particularly the need to be quiet during the day, when his father, now a night porter, sleeps. When Mr. Wright angrily tells Richard to kill a meowing kitten if that's the only way he can keep it quiet, Richard has found a way to strike back without being punished. He takes his father literally and hangs the kitten. But Rich-

ard's mother punishes him by making him bury
the kitten and by filling him with guilt.

Wright now introduces another of his central
themes. When his father deserts the family, young
Richard faces constant and severe hunger. For the
first time, Richard sees himself as different from
others, because he no longer has a father and because he must consequently assume some of the
responsibilities of an adult. Rebellion, hunger, and
the sense of being different will continue with
Richard throughout this book.

In Memphis, Richard's mother teaches him to
fight in self-defense. When he accompanies her to
work at white people's houses, he first senses economic differences, but not yet racial differences.
Some people, he notices, have more to eat than
others. When he doesn't accompany his mother to
work, he amuses himself by spying on people using the open wooden outhouses or by letting saloon patrons ply him with drinks.

But Richard also soon shows his capacity for and
delight in learning, even before he starts school,
which he begins at a later age than other boys because his mother couldn't afford his school clothes.
His first day at school he learns obscene words on
the playground and proudly writes them on the
neighbors' windows. Have knowledge, writing, and
rebellion already become linked for the young
Richard Wright?

Richard's mother goes to court to try to compel
her husband to pay child support. Richard's father
jovially tells the judge that he is doing all he can,
and the judge takes his word for it. Then poverty
compels Richard's mother to send him to an orphanage. There he is given little to eat, forced to

work hard, and deprived of his mother's company. He runs away but is found and returned by white policemen. Note that the policemen give Richard his third chance to learn about whites. His second opportunity came when he heard that a "white" man had beaten a "black" boy. Because Richard's grandmother had light, essentially white, skin, he had never before thought of whites as different from blacks.

NOTE: Wright's maternal grandmother, Margaret Bolden Wilson, had more Irish and Scottish than black ancestry. Born a slave, she did not work in the fields but had the more favored job of a house maid. Though she remained illiterate, after the Civil War she learned the trade of a midwife-nurse and became an assistant to a white doctor.

Now remembering the story of the beating, he is afraid of the white policemen, but they treat him kindly. So far, Richard seems to feel more oppressed by hunger, his delinquent father, and parental punishment than by racism.

At the end of the chapter, Richard's mother takes him to his father's house to ask for money, which request his father refuses. Years later, Richard still thinks back on this disturbing memory of his father sitting by a fire with a strange woman.

NOTE: Many readers point out that during the adolescence Wright describes later in *Black Boy*, he seems to avoid relationships with females. Some

readers link what they see as his avoidance of sexual intimacy to events like this one. After all, they
say, his father's sexual affair meant hunger and
poverty for Richard and his ailing mother. Do you
agree with this interpretation?

Some twenty-five years later, Richard visits his
father again and realizes the gap between the older
man's life and his own. In this passage, Wright
lets you know where *Black Boy* is heading. He sees
his father as a black peasant who has been de-
stroyed by the city and compares his father's life
to his own life, which was to be liberated by the
city. Touching on several of his book's central
themes, Wright refers to his father as a victim of
whites but also calls his father emotionally, as well
as economically, impoverished. Wright's critique
of his fellow blacks has been criticized in turn by
other black writers like James Baldwin.

CHAPTER II

The Wrights move to the home of Richard's Aunt
Maggie. But their pleasant life there ends when
whites kill Maggie's husband. Later the threat of
violence by whites forces Maggie to flee again.

* * *

As the chapter begins, Richard and his family
are moving. Richard's mother insists that he say
good-bye to the other children at the orphanage,
and he does so only to oblige her. From the van-
tage point of later years, Wright reflects on what
he sees as the absence of genuine and deep emotion among blacks, despite stereotypes to the con-
trary. He thinks about the "bleakness" of black life

in America and about the isolation of blacks from the "spirit of Western civilization."

Here, Wright touches on two important points—his sense of isolation and his criticism of the emotional life of blacks. Many readers have attacked Wright on both points and have seen a connection between these two positions. For example, in his essay "The World and the Jug," novelist Ralph Ellison singles out this passage for attack. Ellison and others argue that Wright was indeed isolated from his fellow blacks and complain about his inability to appreciate the richness of black family and community life. Others see Wright's separateness as a natural and desireable quality in a writer. Without this ability to distance himself from the people with whom he grew up, Wright would never have emerged from that community to become a writer of international stature, they maintain. And some people link his critique of the black community to a long tradition of black reformers and radicals, from Booker T. Washington to Malcolm X, who have been critical of traditional black responses to white racism. Which interpretation do you support?

Richard, his mother, and his brother stay for a while in Jackson, Mississippi, at Richard's grandmother's house. Two revealing incidents occur there. Ella, a boarder, reads novels, and Richard demands that she read to him. Though she knows that Granny regards novels as the work of the Devil, Ella reads to Richard from *Bluebeard and His Seven Wives*. Richard's imagination is powerfully aroused, but Granny furiously scolds Ella and slaps Richard. Note that Richard calls this the first experience of his life that provoked a "total emotional response." Does fiction provoke a deeper response from Richard than do the people around him? Remember also that this incident links books and words with sin and rebellion. Finally, notice the resemblance between his first experience with fiction and Wright's own fictional work. *Native Son* has some of the violent and nightmarish qualities that Wright attributes to the tale of *Bluebeard*.

The other incident occurs when Richard is bathing. His grandmother is washing him, and when she scrubs his rectum, he asks her to kiss it. He hasn't realized the meaning of his words, but first Granny and then his mother beat him. Richard again learns the power of words, and once more finds them associated with rebellion and punishment. Granny herself connects the two incidents by blaming Richard's obscenities on Ella's novels.

Wright remembers the pleasant experiences of Jackson, from chasing fireflies to fishing in country creeks.

NOTE: Readers differ in their opinions of these lists of country pleasures. Some praise them for showing that Wright did indeed appreciate the simple life of the black rural South. Others see them as unconvincing compilations that don't change the generally critical thrust of the book. Perhaps their significance lies in their placement. The lists may indicate the few points in Wright's childhood when he was able to enjoy himself. In this way, they heighten the bleakness of the rest of his childhood by contrast. Why do you think Wright included them?

The incidents Wright has selected for most of the rest of the chapter indicate Richard's growing awareness of the South's color line. On the train from Jackson to his Aunt Maggie's house in Elaine, Arkansas, Richard notices that whites and blacks sit in different parts of the train. He questions his mother about his white-looking grandmother. His mother is evasive in her answers to some of his questions. Richard knows that white people sometimes act violently toward blacks. He resolves, that if anyone tries to kill him, he will kill that person first.

At the home of Aunt Maggie and Uncle Hoskins, Richard has more food than ever before. For a while, he hoards biscuits because he's afraid the supply of food will not last. One day, Uncle Hoskins teases him by driving their horse and buggy into the middle of a river. Richard is terrified, and the terror creates a permanent barrier between him and Hoskins. (Notice how rare it is that Richard does not feel a barrier between himself and others.)

One night Uncle Hoskins does not return from work at the saloon he owns. He has been shot and killed by whites who want to take over his business. They threaten to kill his family also, so Maggie, Richard, and Richard's mother and brother flee to the town of West Helena. Maggie is not even able to see her husband's body or to claim any of his assets. Soon thereafter, the family moves back to Granny's in Jackson.

Once more young Richard is uprooted, and once more he is poor. Though this incident marks the first time that racism has directly affected Richard, note how significant the incident is. It seems reasonable to expect that if Uncle Hoskins had been allowed to stay in business, Richard's family would have had a stable home. They might have enjoyed independence from his grandmother's household and from her religious extremism, and maintained a decent standard of living. Though racism was not the only cause of the hardships of Wright's childhood, the murder of Uncle Hoskins may certainly be evidence that racism played a crucial role in preventing the Wright family from overcoming their problems. What problems besides racism affected young Richard's life?

While at Granny's, Richard sees a chain gang and notices that the prisoners are black and the guards white. Some time thereafter, his family moves back to West Helena to escape from Granny's strict religious rules.

NOTE: Seventh-Day Adventism Granny is a Seventh-Day Adventist. The religion takes its name from the belief that the second coming of Christ and the end of the world (the Advent) are near and from its celebration of the Sabbath on the seventh day of the week, Saturday. Seventh-Day Adventism was the religion of only a small minority of Southerners. Most blacks were Baptists or Methodists (like Wright's mother). Seventh-Day Adventism demanded that its adherents eat no pork and that they not work on Saturdays. Both were difficult rules for poor Southern blacks to abide by. Saturday work was important to low-paid blacks, and pork was the most common meat in the Southern diet.

Back in West Helena, Richard and the other

neighborhood children amuse themselves by chanting insults at the Jew who owns the grocery store. On another occasion, Richard peers into the neighboring flat and sees a couple making love. That apartment is in fact a brothel owned by the landlady. As a result of Richard's spying, his family has to move again.

Richard is introduced to a new uncle, Professor Matthews. One night Matthews and Aunt Maggie flee hurriedly. Though Richard knows none of the details, it appears that Matthews has robbed and killed a white woman. With Aunt Maggie no longer there to contribute to the household income, Richard is hungry most of the time.

Matthews had given Richard a poodle. He takes it to a white neighborhood to sell it. Richard offers to sell the dog for a dollar, but then he finds an excuse to back out of the deal. He doesn't want to sell her to white people.

The chapter ends by touching both on the book's social themes and on its psychological and personal issues. Richard hears stories about racial conflict and black vengeance, and comes to dread whites and to imagine himself standing up to them with violence. But he also feels that he is living mainly in a world of his imagination, the only place where he can find the satisfactions denied him by his bleak life. In the chapter's last paragraphs, Richard again looks at what appears to be a bird in the sky. Af first he doesn't believe the people who tell him he is looking at an airplane in which people fly. This image of flight and freedom contrasts with his miserable Christmas. His only gift is one orange, which he saves until nighttime.

CHAPTER III

Richard's mother has a stroke. Richard is sent to his Uncle Clark's, but he is unhappy there and insists on returning to his mother's.

* * *

Richard hangs out with the other black boys of the neighborhood. They talk about many things, but Wright emphasizes their conversations about whites. They talk about white folks' meanness and brag about what they will do to them. And they have vicious fights with the white boys who enter the black neighborhood.

Some readers think that Wright always remains aloof from the black community. But others point to this chapter, where Richard appears as an integral part of his peer group. Note that a major basis of their solidarity seems to be their need to defend themselves against whites.

Richard's mother becomes too ill to work. Richard has to take odd jobs, and the family, often unable to pay its rent, must move frequently from one part of town to another. One morning Richard awakens to find his mother paralyzed. She has suffered a stroke. In evaluating the aftermath of this catastrophe, you may find three things especially significant. First, note that Richard's mother seems to be the only person to whom he feels a strong emotional attachment. Her illness and possibly imminent death are devastatingly frightening to him. Second, note that, though Wright doesn't dwell on it, the response to his mother's illness suggests a strong community and family solidarity. Until Granny arrives and takes the family with her to Jackson, the neighbors nurse Richard's mother and feed the children. Then, at Granny's request, six of her eight other children descend upon Jackson to help. In evaluating Wright's portrait of the black family and the black community, remember this incident as well as the ones in which he is more critical. Finally, his mother's illness intensifies Wright's withdrawal from the people around him. Could Wright's placement of this incident immediately after a rare description of his easy-going friendship with his peers suggest that his mother's sudden illness prevented his continuing what might otherwise have become a more normal social life?

Richard has nightmares, and he sleepwalks. His brother is sent to live with Aunt Maggie in Detroit. Richard would have liked to go with Maggie, but, deprived of that possibility, he chooses to stay with Uncle Clark in Greenwood, because it is only a few miles from Jackson. His aunt and uncle give him food, clothing, and shelter but little affection. When Richard learns that another child died in the bed in which he is sleeping, fear keeps him awake at night. He insists on returning to Jackson.

In Jackson, his mother has an operation. Because there are no hospital facilities for blacks, friendly white doctors help smuggle her in and out wrapped in bandages. She shows no sign of improving, however. His mother's suffering becomes for Wright a symbol of all the pain and suffering of his life. Wright says that her illness set the emotional tone of the rest of his life, forever on the move and forever separate from other people. He says that it helped give him the conviction that he had to "wring" his life's meaning "out of meaningless suffering."

NOTE: Wright's description of his future is also accurate as a description of his life after writing *Black Boy*. His wanderings continued. He left the United States for Paris, just as he had previously left the South for the North and Chicago for New York. In Paris he became an adherent of the philosophical school known as existentialism, an outlook on life that stresses the isolation and spiritual suffering of the individual and that places upon the individual the responsibility for creating the meaning of his own life.

CHAPTER IV

Richard confronts his Aunt Addie, who teaches at the Seventh-Day Adventist church school. He also resists his grandmother's attempts to convert him to religious faith. And he writes his first story.

* * *

Richard finds himself in a delicate position in Granny's household. He is a child and an uninvited one at that. He is also a nonbeliever. Granny even suggests that his disbelief is responsible for his mother's illness. In addition to the tension over religion, Richard is always hungry at Granny's. Meals usually consist either of mush with lard and flour gravy, or greens with lard.

Richard is forced to enter the Adventist religious school, and is taught by his Aunt Addie. He finds the pupils boring and docile. One day Addie accuses him of eating walnuts in class. She beats him brutally for this offense, which he didn't commit, and for calling her Aunt Addie instead of Mrs.

Wilson. At home she is about to beat him again, but he fights back and threatens to use a knife. He feels that he has won a victory. Subsequently, Addie rarely even speaks to him.

Despite Richard's hostility to the strict religious environment around him, do you think that his upbringing in a religious home influenced him nonetheless? He writes of the sermons' vivid language, of religion's "dramatic vision" of a life always influenced by the thought of death, of its appealing sense of fate.

NOTE: In an unpublished essay called "Memories of My Grandmother," Wright further supports the idea that religion had some positive influence on him. He criticizes his grandmother for her insensitivity to individuals and her loyalty to an abstract ideal. But he also says that her religious precepts taught him to live "beyond the world . . . to be *in* the world but not *of* the world (Wright's italics)."

A family campaign begins, with the goal of converting Richard. Granny, Aunt Addie, and even his friends beg him to come to God. Richard has no intention of complying but does not want these people to hate him. One day he inadvertently embarrasses Granny in church. He tells her that he will convert if he sees an angel. Of course, he is confident that he will never see one. But she thinks he's saying that he *has* seen an angel, and she tells the other church members. She is deeply disillusioned when she finds out the truth.

Richard pretends to spend time praying but cannot. Instead, one day he writes a story about an Indian maiden and reads it to a girl next door. She is baffled by it, and he cherishes her perplexed reaction. Note that Richard writes this story in the aftermath of his family's attempt to convert him. Is this timing evidence that the religious teachings have influenced him after all, though, of course, not in a way that the family had intended? Has all the other-worldly religious talk helped him write this other-worldly story? Or, on the other hand, is his writing another result of his rebellion. Remember that his religious family thought fiction to be the work of the Devil. Knowing what you do about Richard, which interpretation do you favor?

CHAPTER V

Richard gets a job selling newspapers but quits when he finds that the newspapers espouse racist views. Later, his grandfather dies.

* * *

Granny and Aunt Addie have given up on Richard. He returns to public school, where he proves himself to the other boys by fighting with the school's toughest bullies. This schooling is his first opportunity for uninterrupted study, and he does surprisingly well. In two weeks he is promoted from fifth to sixth grade. But he cannot fully mingle with his classmates because of his grandmother's religious objections to his working on Saturdays. With no spending money, he has to stand apart at lunch time, and he lies about his reasons for not eating. Note Richard's desire to be part of a group and his inability to fulfill that desire.

A friend suggests that he sell newspapers in the evenings. By doing so, he earns some spending money, and he also reads the horror and adventure stories in the paper's magazine supplement. But a friend of the family shows him that the newspaper itself is violently racist. Richard is shocked because the papers come from Chicago, the city to which many Southern blacks are fleeing. The friend tells Richard that he has been selling Ku Klux Klan literature, and Richard gives up his paper route. Racism has again affected Richard's chances for happiness.

NOTE: The Ku Klux Klan is a racist group founded after the Civil War. Its purpose was to restore white supremacy in the South, where, for a while, blacks were beginning to attain some political power. Later the group continued its anti-black agitation and violence, while also opposing other nonwhite groups, as well as Jews and immigrants.

During that summer Richard has another nearly violent confrontation with Addie. He threatens her with a knife. Looking back, Wright comments that instead of bringing peace, the religion of his home seemed to cause constant strife.

Richard gets a summer job accompanying an agent on his trips to sell burial insurance to sharecroppers (tenant farmers). He realizes how worldly and urban he is compared to the sharecroppers. Already, Wright has a sense of the distance between himself and the world of his roots, a distance that will only grow deeper as he grows older.

In this section Wright seems to find nothing of value in the lives of rural Southern blacks. They are "a bare, bleak pool" of people who are all "alike." (Passages like this one have been criticized by Baldwin, Ellison, and others who feel that Wright was not sympathetic enough to the vitality of black community life.)

Richard's grandfather dies. Although he had fought in the Civil War, he had been denied a pension because his discharge papers had misspelled his name. For the rest of his life he had tried and failed to have this mistake corrected.

Richard threatens to leave home if he can't work on Saturdays. Under that threat, his grandmother relents, and his sick mother is pleased that he has defied his grandmother and aunt. Note the continuing importance of Wright's mother. His rebellion is not directed at her and in fact seems to have her approval.

CHAPTER VI

Richard gets a job working for white people. Then he is baptized in his mother's church. Finally, he has another near-violent confrontation with a relative.

* * *

For the first time, Richard is spending much time among whites, as a result of Granny's allowing him to work. At his first job interview, a woman asks him if he steals. After he gets the job doing house work, Richard works hard but discovers that his food is stale bread and moldy molasses. The woman employing him expresses surprise that a black boy would have any interest in staying in school, so he tells her of his ambition to be a writer. She wonders who put such crazy ideas in his head, and he decides to look for work elsewhere.

He doesn't like his next employer much better, and reflecting on these events, Wright wonders if he would have resented whites as much if he had entered the white world earlier and become used to their insults.

Richard also feels that he is excluded from the community life of the black world around him. He longs to participate, but he feels that he has already become too different from the others. He attends Sunday School, and the other students urge him to become a member of his mother's Methodist church. At one church service, he is pressured into agreeing to become baptized. The minister creates a situation where refusing baptism would mean rejecting his own mother in front of the entire congregation. Thus, he gives in, but religion still seems meaningless to him.

Because the family needs money, Uncle Tom and his family move in. One morning, Tom thinks that Richard has been rude to him and prepares to beat him. Richard will not let himself be beaten by a man who is almost a stranger to him. He threatens Tom with razor blades and forces him to back off. Tom tells Richard that he will end up on the gallows, but Richard tells Tom that he will never lead a life as degrading as Tom's.

Note how this chapter shows Richard oppressed by both the black and white worlds around him. Both have an image of how he should behave, and Wright seems to imply that the two images are not so different. For example, he says that Tom wants to beat him for not acting like the "backward" black boys on the plantations. Like Richard's white employer, Tom is sure that Richard will never amount to anything.

Some readers think that Wright's portrayal of his fellow blacks is unfair. They also question whether he was in the right as often as he portrays himself. Where, they ask, could he have learned such integrity if the world around him was so devoid of it? Others think his criticism perceptive and courageous. They feel that he gives sufficient indication of the sources of his rebellious attitudes. For example, though he disagrees with his grandmother, he resembles her in stubbornly choosing a path that is not that of the majority. Which viewpoint do you think is more valid? Why?

NOTE: Thomas Wilson Richard Wright's uncle, Thomas Wilson, was an unemployed teacher, who earned a living repairing furniture. Some readers feel that Wright was not sympathetic enough to a man who was doing his best under difficult circumstances. Wilson was already suffering the beginnings of Parkinson's disease, a chronic and progressive nervous disease that weakens muscles and causes tremors. And, though Wright doesn't mention it in *Black Boy*, his uncle's occupational situation was soon to improve. Uncle Thomas became a real estate broker and later wrote a book on the word "Negro." He made a substantial amount of money and became a community leader. Moreover, he and Wright became friendly in later years.

CHAPTER VII

Richard publishes his first story. The reaction
from his family is overwhelmingly negative.

* * *

Richard gets a job carrying water to thirsty workers at a brick yard. The boss's dog bites him, and
the boss laughs, saying that a dog bite can't hurt
a black. School is about to begin again, and Richard expects the year to be bleak. He wonders why
everyone but himself accepts authority and tradition.

One afternoon, while bored in class, Richard
writes a story, which he calls "The Voodoo of Hell's
Half-Acre." He submits it to the local black newspaper, and the editor prints it in three install-
ments. Richard finds that far from admiring him
for the story, his classmates are perplexed and suspicious.

At home the reaction is even worse. His grandmother calls the story a lie and the Devil's work.
His mother thinks it will hurt his chances of ob-
taining a teaching job. Uncle Tom finds the story
pointless, and Aunt Addie thinks the use of the
word "hell" is a sin. Once more, writing seems to
be a crime. Looking back, Wright notes that he was
harboring ambitions that the entire system of
Southern racism was designed to stifle. But note
that the people most strongly opposed to him are
fellow blacks. Is Wright suggesting that most blacks
acquiesced in and even enforced some aspects of
Southern racism?

NOTE: Biographers of Wright have interviewed
the typesetter at the paper that published this story.

She claims that the story, published in spring of 1924 in the *Southern Register*, was titled "Hell's Half Acre" and that it was an account of personal experiences rather than the heavily imaginative and atmospheric tale that Wright remembers. She also says that the story's hero was a boy named Bigger Thomas, Wright's childhood friend who became one of the models for the hero of *Native Son*.

CHAPTER VIII

Richard becomes class valedictorian. But he refuses to give the speech written for him by the principal.

* * *

Richard hears that a classmate's brother has been killed by whites for visiting a white prostitute. Richard realizes how afraid he is of the white terror that could assault him at any time.

The hostility he feels at home seems to be intensifying too. He discovers that Uncle Tom has admonished his children not to associate with Richard. When Richard's brother returns home from Aunt Maggie's, he joins in the criticism of Richard.

At the end of the ninth-grade school term, Richard is chosen valedictorian. The principal hands him a speech to recite, but Richard writes his own speech. He insists on reading it, and neither the principal nor his friends, family, and classmates can dissuade him. Once more his writing has become an offense. And once again the black community is cooperating in keeping him down.

NOTE: Wright modified this incident slightly when he wrote *Black Boy*. His speech concerned the way in which the Southern educational system stunted the intellectual development of the black population. While he did insist on reading it against the opposition he describes in the book, he also consented to cut certain passages. In addition, Wright does not mention that the principal had just received permission to start a new school for blacks, a high school that would go beyond the customary ninth grade. Thus, the principal feared any controversy that would jeopardize this project. Of course, keep in mind that this fear does not necessarily justify his act of censorship nor invalidate Wright's criticism of the principal and of the system within which he was working. How severely would you criticize the principal? Would you criticize Wright at all? Why?

CHAPTER IX

Richard has several terrifying confrontations with whites. In the most important of these confrontations, he is forced out of a job because he dares to ask to learn the skills of the trade.

* * *

After graduating from the ninth grade, Richard gets a job in a clothing store. One day his employers beat a black woman for not paying her bills. Later, some white men offer him a ride into town but beat him when he forgets to call them "sir." Then his boss fires him because he doesn't like the look in Richard's eyes.

One of Richard's friends has some advice for him. He should learn how to live as a black man in the South. He must hide his true feelings and always remember to act differently in front of white people than he does with blacks. He must think before he speaks to whites.

The friend helps Richard find a job in an optical company run by a Northerner. The Northerner introduces Richard to Pease and Reynolds, two skilled workers who will, he says, help him learn the trade of grinding lenses. They are friendly to him, but their attitude changes when he asks them to tell him about the skilled work. One day they put him in an impossible situation. Reynolds says that he heard Richard call Pease, "Pease," rather than "Mr. Pease." If Richard denies this charge, he is calling Reynolds a liar. If he admits it, he is insulting Pease. Either way, the men threaten to kill him. He knows they want him to quit the job, so he does.

Richard feels that his friend's advice has done him no good. The Northern boss calls him in and tries to bring him back to work. But Richard knows that if he accuses the men, they may well kill him. His hopes are dashed, and he is crying. He knows he will have to leave the South.

NOTE: Some biographers of Wright think that he worked for the optical company in the summer after eighth grade and that he left the job only in order to return to school. However, the two white employees did threaten and harass him because of his desire to learn the trade.

CHAPTER X

Richard learns to steal. By stealing he acquires enough money to leave the Deep South.

* * *

Richard sees Pease and Reynolds not as individuals but as part of "a huge, implacable, elemental design." Richard is determined to adapt to the white world. His next job is in a drugstore, where his efforts to behave properly make him so tense that he fails at trivial tasks and is fired.

Richard feels that he has to learn ways of acting that seem automatic for other blacks. Has Richard's isolation within the black community made his dealings with white society more difficult too?

He gets a job at a hotel. While working, he observes the other blacks there. He believes they have blocked from their consciousness all thoughts and feelings banned by whites, and he calls their lives "debased." Once more Richard seems to show little sympathy for the Southern black community. How likely do you think it was that all of Wright's companions could have been so completely brainwashed by the harsh and discriminatory conditions of their lives? Remember that Wright was only one of many blacks to flee the South.

Richard considers stealing to obtain the money he needs to leave Mississippi. He knows that many blacks steal, and he disapproves. He'd rather see them unite and ask for their rights. The whites like blacks to steal because it confirms their belief that blacks are irresponsible. But Richard also feels that if whites don't act lawfully toward him, he doesn't need to respect the law in his dealings with them. He starts to sell liquor, sales of which were illegal

at the time. Then he takes a job selling tickets at a
movie theater and joins a scheme to resell the tickets and pocket the money. Finally, he steals and
sells a neighbor's gun and some cans of preserves
in the college storehouse.

NOTE:　Compare Richard's attitude to crime to
Bigger's in *Native Son*. Both seem to gain a sense
of freedom from their crimes and to see them as
acts of rebellion against the white world. But Wright
is no Bigger Thomas. His crime has a specific purpose and when he has raised the money he needs
to leave, he knows that he will never steal again.

CHAPTER XI

Richard finds a place to stay in Memphis. The
owner of his rooming house encourages him to
marry her daughter.

* * *

Richard has gone to Memphis, where he finds
a room in a rooming house. Mrs. Moss, his landlady, is warm and friendly, and Richard is startled
at the difference between her and his family. She
invites him to dinner and introduces him to her
daughter, Bess. Mrs. Moss soon hints that Richard
should marry Bess. He is astonished at this behavior from someone he has just met. That night Bess
sits with Richard in the front room. She kisses him
and tells him that she loves him. He responds to
her kisses and is amazed again when he contrasts
these women with Aunt Addie. But when he tells

Bess that they should get to know each other better first, she runs away, hurt.

In Memphis, Richard seems to be learning two things: that his experience has been limited and that he is indeed incapable of breaking out of his isolation and engaging himself with others. Do you think Richard is also revealing a degree of sexual inhibition? His whole life history to date may suggest a shyness with women, though this theme is not one that Wright raises explicitly.

CHAPTER XII

Richard takes another job with an optical company. The foreman tries to provoke a fight between him and a black employee of another company.

* * *

Richard's experience at the optical company in Jackson enables him to obtain a job at a similar firm in Memphis. By comparison to Jackson, he finds race relations in Tennessee relaxed. He works hard, runs errands at lunch for tips, and skimps on food in order to save enough to have his mother and brother join him. He reads much too, but now he reads literary magazines instead of detective stories.

If race relations are not as tense as in Mississippi, however, they are still his major source of trouble. Wright relates three incidents that illustrate the racial situation in Memphis. The first story concerns a fellow black worker named Shorty, an intelligent and proud man. Around whites, however, he plays the clown. For example, one day he asks a white man for a quarter and in return lets the man kick him in the pants. But Wright comments that all his fellow workers cared more about bread than about dignity.

The second incident occurs when a Northerner approaches Richard and asks him if he is hungry. Richard is indeed hungry, but he would be ashamed to admit it. The Northerner offers him a dollar, which he wants but refuses. The Northerner may mean well, but he doesn't understand the feelings of the person to whom he is talking.

The third incident begins when Richard's foreman tells him that Harrison, a black man who works across the street, plans to stab him after work. Richard talks to Harrison and discovers that the foreman has told Harrison that Richard is planning to stab *him*. Apparently, the foreman is trying to provoke them into attacking each other. Whatever the foreman may be up to, the two young men are suspicious of each other nonetheless. A week later, the foreman suggests the two settle their "grudge" by boxing. Harrison persuades Richard to accept, and they agree not to hurt each other. Once in the ring, however, they go for blood and vent on each other all the hatred they feel for the whites who put them up to this sport.

Apparently, the racism in Memphis, though less pervasive, can be quite vicious after all, just as Wright will later find out about the racism in Chicago. But note also that Wright does not glorify his own behavior here. Although some readers criticize Wright for portraying his own actions too favorably, here he freely admits his weaknesses.

NOTE: Biographers are uncertain whether this particular fight ever took place, but whites definitely did stage fights between blacks in a similar manner. One of the famous scenes in modern literature is the "battle royal" among a group of young black boys in Ralph Ellison's *Invisible Man*. There the boys beat each other up for the amusement of their white audience.

CHAPTER XIII

Richard borrows a library card and discovers the hard-hitting style of columnist H.L. Mencken. He begins to read voraciously.

* * *

While reading the Memphis newspaper, Richard comes across an editorial attacking H.L. Mencken. He decides that if a Southern newspaper attacks a white man, that man might be worth reading. Blacks aren't allowed to borrow books from the public library, so Richard must use a white's library card. The only white he feels he can approach is a Catholic, who is hated by his fellow Southerners because of his religion. Richard succeeds in borrowing the Catholic's card and forges a note to the librarian asking her to give "this nigger boy" some books by Mencken.

Richard is shocked by Mencken's style. He realizes that Mencken uses words as weapons and wonders if he can do the same. The preoccupations of *Black Boy* with racism and with Wright's development as a writer merge here. Richard is attracted to Mencken because a newspaper that usually attacks black people has attacked Mencken. In reading Mencken, his desire to fight back against whites and his desire to write stories fuse for what appears to be the first time. But, of course, as you may have already noticed, words and rebellion have been connected before in Richard's life, at least as early as the day he wrote obscenities on his neighbors' windows.

Richard reads Sinclair Lewis, Theodore Dreiser, and some of the other authors Mencken discusses. He develops a passion for reading, but he worries that his reading will antagonize the whites around him. Whites think that reading makes blacks rebellious. Richard's hunger becomes a hunger to understand life and people and to become capable of writing about them.

Richard's mother and brother arrive in Memphis. Richard feels his reading has isolated him even further from Southern life. He reviews all the options open to Southern blacks. He can rebel, but then he will be killed. He can submit, perhaps marry Bess, but he considers that choice a form of slavery. He can use his restless energy to fight other blacks. Or he can lose himself in sex and alcohol like his father did.

NOTE: *Native Son* also reviews a similar range of alternatives for Chicago blacks. Bigger's girlfriend Bessie loses herself in sex and alcohol; in the early portion of the book, Bigger turns his angry energy upon other blacks; later Bigger rebels and is killed; Bigger's mother submits and doesn't challenge the conditions of her life.

CHAPTER XIV

Richard leaves for Chicago.

* * *

Deserted by her new husband, Aunt Maggie visits Memphis. The family decides that Richard and Maggie will leave for Chicago. When Richard tells his boss that he is leaving, he says that his departure is at his family's insistence. The white men at the factory are uneasy about a black man who wants to go north. They seem to consider that desire an implicit criticism of the South and thus of them.

On the train north, Richard reflects on his life. He wonders how he came to believe that life could be lived more fully. Where did he get his desire to escape? His answer is that he acquired this desire from books. The books he read were critical of America and suggested that the country could be reshaped for the better.

Is Richard's answer accurate? Wright seems to have wanted a different and better life long before he discovered Mencken and the other writers he read in Memphis. Can you shape a more complex answer to Wright's question from the information he has provided in *Black Boy?*

Richard continues his reflections. He thinks the white South has allowed him only one honest path, that of rebellion. He argues to himself that the white South, and his own family, conforming to the dictates of whites, have not let him develop more than a portion of his personality. Yet he also thinks he is taking with him a part of the South. How will it bloom, he wonders, in different soil?

Here Wright focuses on the way his life in the South has been typical of other black lives, all stunted by racism. In this conclusion, Wright doesn't dwell so much on the uniqueness of his life. In fact, for the first time, he stresses that he is a product of the South and must be accepted as such. Do you agree?

A STEP BEYOND

Test and Answers

TEST

1. Richard sets fire to   _____
   A. his house   B. a white man's house
   C. his neighbor's house

2. Granny often speaks of   _____
   A. God   B. the books she reads
   C. her love for her grandchildren

3. Richard accepts baptism   _____
   I. to avoid humiliation
   II. to please his mother
   III. to please God
   A. II and III only   B. I and III only
   C. I and II only

4. Richard leaves his first job with an optical   _____
   company because
   A. he finds a better job
   B. the work is too demanding
   C. the other employees threaten him

5. In Memphis, Richard discovers   _____
   A. the Communist Party
   B. the works of H.L. Mencken
   C. the woman of his dreams

6. Richard thinks that the principal of his   _____
   school is a

    A. genius   B. madman   C. coward

7. Uncle Hoskins is killed by white people who   _____
    A. envy his business
    B. mistake him for someone else
    C. think he is a Communist

8. When Richard's father deserts his family,   _____
    A. Richard tries to convince him to come back
    B. the family must get by with little to eat
    C. Richard's mother takes a lover

9. Richard's first published story is called   _____
    A. "Big Boy Leaves Home"
    B. "The Man Who Lived Underground"
    C. "The Voodoo of Hell's Half-Acre"

10. When Uncle Tom tries to beat Richard, the   _____ boy
    A. slits his attacker's throat
    B. threatens him with razor blades
    C. bursts into tears

11. Is *Black Boy* more an indictment of Southern racism or an account of a writer's development? Explain.

12. What positive and what negative lessons does Richard learn from his fellow blacks?

Answers

1. A   2. A   3. C   4. C   5. B   6. C
7. A   8. B   9. C   10. B

11. Certainly the later chapters of the book focus on Richard's experiences with white racists. But even the earlier portions touch on the theme of racism. Uncle

Hoskins' death is more than just a shocking example of racist violence. It also changes Richard's life by depriving him of the stable home and economic prosperity that he was beginning to enjoy. The book's conclusion confirms that its subject is racism: Richard flees the South because he can no longer endure its discriminatory practices.

On the other hand, Wright directs much of his criticism against his own family and his fellow blacks. Many of the hardships of his early life stem from his grandmother's strictness. Even before Richard's writing ambitions develop into an explicit theme, he is using words in a rebellious way. You could argue that many of the obstacles he encounters would be set in the way of any sensitive and critical individual who questions society's codes. In addition, you could say that the ending of *Black Boy* confirms that Wright's development into a writer is the book's central theme. After all, he does not leave the South until he decides upon his career.

12. Wright is often critical of his fellow blacks. He learns from them how not to act. For example, he learns to avoid his father's irresponsible sexual affairs. He rebels against religion. He decides not to follow the principal's compromising path to a position of professional responsibility. He doesn't want to play the buffoon in front of whites as Shorty does or even to defer to whites like his other friends do. On the other hand, he is fascinated by the biblical stories he hears in his family's church in much the same way as he is drawn to the story of Bluebeard. In addition, he may have acquired his stubborn insistence on following his own path from his grandmother's equally strong determination to do what she thinks right even when the rest of the world is doing something else. His mother's ability to endure suffering may have inspired him to persevere even in the face of adversity. Finally, some of his friends teach him how to survive in the white world and, although he may not entirely like their lessons, he heeds them in order to cope with life.

Native Son
&
Black Boy

Term Paper Ideas
and other
Topics for Writing

Characters

1. Compare the character of Bigger Thomas in *Native Son* to that of the young Richard Wright in *Black Boy*.

2. Which of *Native Son*'s subsidiary characters are convincing to you, and which aren't? Why?

3. Use psychological and sociological studies of black rage to evaluate the validity of Wright's characterization of Bigger.

4. Is the young Richard Wright of *Black Boy* only a rebel against his family or is he also a product of that family's influences in a more positive sense too? Explain.

5. Does Wright succeed in making Bigger a sympathetic character? Is that his goal? Explain.

Themes

1. Compare Wright's attitude toward the black church in *Native Son* and in *Black Boy*. Does he criticize only or does he see a positive dimension too? What evidence can you offer?

2. Evaluate James Baldwin's critique of Richard Wright in the essays "Many Thousands Gone," "Everybody's Protest Novel," and "Poor Richard." Is Baldwin correct in his criticism of Wright's portrayal of black community life?

3. How does Wright view male-female relationships? Draw evidence from both *Native Son* and *Black Boy*.

4. Is *Black Boy* primarily an indictment of Southern racism, or is it primarily the story of an artist's coming of age? Explain.

5. Evaluate today's mass media in the light of Wright's critique in *Native Son*. Are any of his criticisms still valid? What has changed?

Style, Setting, and Structure

1. Identify the patterns of imagery in *Native Son*. How do they affect the novel's atmosphere and its meaning?

2. What did Wright gain and what did he lose in narrating *Native Son* from Bigger's point of view?

3. How does Wright use setting symbolically in *Native Son*?

4. What are the turning points in Richard's development in *Black Boy*?

History

1. How much of *Native Son*'s ideas come from the Communist Party of Wright's time? How do *Native Son*'s ideas differ from those of the Communist Party?

2. How accurate was Wright's portrayal of the racism of his time? What is your evidence?

3. What are *Native Son*'s literary roots? Consider both the tradition of literary naturalism and that of the Gothic horror story.

Evaluation

1. Do you find *Native Son* too melodramatic? Explain.

2. Does the case Max makes for Bigger convince you? Would it be likely to convince a judge? How would you argue Bigger's case?

3. Is *Native Son* dated? Is it still meaningful and relevant? Which parts do you find dated and which still relevant?

Further Reading
CRITICAL WORKS

Abcarian, Richard, ed. *Richard Wright's Native Son: A Critical Handbook*. Belmont, California: Wadsworth, 1970. Includes several good reviews and essays.

Baker, Houston A., Jr., ed. *Twentieth Century Interpretations of Native Son: A Collection of Critical Essays*. Englewood Cliffs, N.J.: Prentice-Hall, 1972. Includes some of the most controversial essays on *Native Son*.

Bakish, David. *Richard Wright*. New York: Frederick Ungar, 1973.

Brignano, Russell Carl. *Richard Wright: An Introduction to the Man and His Works*. Pittsburgh: University of Pittsburgh Press, 1970. Organized thematically.

Fabre, Michel. *The Unfinished Quest of Richard Wright*. New York: William Morrow, 1973. The most comprehensive biography of Wright.

Felgar, Robert. *Richard Wright*. Boston: Twayne, 1980. Sees Bigger as a brutalized and degraded character.

Gayle, Addison. *Richard Wright: Ordeal of a Native Son*. Garden City, N.Y.: Doubleday, 1980. Uses newly discovered documents.

Kinnamon, Keneth. *The Emergence of Richard Wright: A Study in Literature and Society*. Urbana: University of Illinois Press, 1972. Emphasizes the influences of Wright's social and political milieu on his literary career.

McCall, Dan. *The Example of Richard Wright*. New York: Harcourt, Brace, 1969. Emphasizes the nightmarish elements of *Native Son*.

Macksey, Richard, and Frank E. Moorer, eds. *Richard Wright: A Collection of Critical Essays*. Englewood Cliffs, N.J.: Prentice-Hall, 1984. Includes more recent essays than other collections.

Ray, David, and Robert M. Farnsworth, eds. *Richard Wright: Impressions and Perspectives*. Ann Arbor: University of Michigan Press, 1973. Includes letters and personal remembrances as well as critical comments.

Reilly, John M., ed. *Richard Wright: The Critical Reception*. New York: Burt Franklin, 1978. Compiles contemporary reviews of all Wright's books.

AUTHOR'S OTHER MAJOR WORKS

For a complete bibliography that includes Wright's poetry, short stories in magazines, essays, book reviews, prefaces to other writers' books, journalism, and correspondence, see Michel Fabre's biography.

1938	*Uncle Tom's Children: Four Novellas*
1941	*Twelve Million Black Voices: A Folk History of the Negro in the United States*
1953	*The Outsider*

1954   *Savage Holiday*
1954   *Black Power: A Record of Reactions in a Land*
            of Pathos
1956   *The Color Curtain*
1956   *Pagan Spain*
1957   *White Man, Listen!*
1958   *The Long Dream*
1961   *Eight Men*
1963   *Lawd Today*

The Critics

On Bigger

Bigger has no discernible relationship to himself, to his own life, to his own people, nor to any other people—in this respect, perhaps, he is most American—and his force comes not from his significance as a social (or anti-social) unit, but from his significance as the incarnation of a myth. It is remarkable that, though we follow him step by step from the tenement room to the death cell, we know as little about him when this journey is ended as we did when it began; and, what is even more remarkable, we know almost as little about the social dynamic which we are to believe created him.

> —James Baldwin, "Many
> Thousands Gone," reprinted in
> *Twentieth-Century Interpretations*
> *of Native Son*, 1972

On the Tone of *Native Son*

Native Son, though preserving some of the devices of the naturalistic novel, deviates sharply from its characteristic tone: a tone Wright could not possibly have maintained and which, it may be, no Negro novelist can really hold for long. *Native Son* is a work of assault rather than withdrawal; the author yields himself in part to a vision of nightmare. Bigger's cowering perception of the world becomes the most vivid and authentic component of the book. Naturalism pushed to an extreme turns here into something other than itself, a kind of expressionist outburst, no longer a replica of the familiar social world but a self-contained realm of grotesque emblems.

> —Irving Howe, "Black Boys and
> Native Sons," reprinted in
> *Twentieth-Century Interpretations
> of Native Son*, 1972

Throughout, the physical description that Wright rushes by us makes us feel the emotional force of the objects but not see them with any real accuracy: we are aware of the furnace and storm as poles of the imagination—fire and ice—in a world of symbolic presences. Continually the world is transformed into a kind of massive skull, and the people are figments of that skull's imagination.

> —Dan McCall, *The Example of
> Richard Wright*, 1969

On Max's Speech

But Max represents the type of so-called legal defense which the Communist Party and the I.L.D. have been fighting, dating from Scottsboro. Some of his speech is mystical, unconvincing, and expresses the point of view held not by the Communists but by those reformist betrayers who are being displaced by the Communists. He accepts the idea that Negroes have a criminal psychology as the book erroneously tends to symbolize in Bigger. He does not challenge the false charge of rape against Bigger, though Bigger did not rape Mary, and though this is the eternal bourbon slander flung against Negroes. He does not deal with the heinous murder of Bessie, tending to accept the bourbon policy that crimes of Negroes against each other don't matter and are not cut from the same capitalist cloth.

> —Ben Davis, Jr., *Sunday Worker*,
> April 14, 1940, reprinted in
> *Richard Wright: The Critical
> Reception*, 1978

Max, in his image of the American people proceeding to their doom like sleepwalkers, catches up these images of darkness present on all sides. It is this blindness that he emphasizes throughout his speech. If the judge reacts only to what he has to say about the sufferings of Negroes, he states, he will be "blinded" by a feeling that will prevent him from perceiving reality and acting accordingly. "Rather, I plead with you to see . . . an existence of men growing out of the soil prepared by the collective but blind will of a hundred million people" (p. 328). "Your Honor," he exclaims, "in our blindness we have so contrived and ordered the lives of men" (p. 336) that their every human aspiration constitutes a threat to the state.

—Paul N. Siegel, "The Conclusion of Richard Wright's Native Son," reprinted in *Richard Wright: A Collection of Critical Essays,* 1984

On Black Boy

Black Boy clarifies the nature of Wright's importance. In any strictly literary sense, he broke no new ground, established no new devices or techniques or methods. He did not make us see our experience in new ways; he made us see new experience. He had a perception about America, a perception of a part of America that was unknown territory. His importance is not really literary but what we should call cultural. We come to him not for new ways of saying things but for the new things he has to say. When he does get "literary" on us, when he draws himself up into "writing," he is merely fancy, and he fails. He would say of his effort in *Black Boy,* "If I could fasten the mind of the reader upon words so firmly that he would forget words and be conscious only of his response, I felt that I would be in sight of knowing how to write narrative. I strove to master words, to make them disappear. . . ." His ability to do that is a major achievement of *Black Boy,* a book virtually uncontaminated by his old rhetoric. In *Native Son* there was too much forensic slag, too many set pieces, a prose racing in all directions, and an explanatory moral. Five years later, Wright has freed himself of his revolutionary slogans and all that went with them; he has grown into his craft and his sense of his life's meaning.

—Dan McCall, *The Example of*
Richard Wright, 1969